WHATEVER YOUR DILEMMA,

THE WRITE WAY

HAS THE ANSWERS....

❏ Anyone who wants to be labeled as sexist please raise *his* hand. Anyone who wants to be labeled as tedious please raise *his or her* hand. Anyone who wants to be labeled as ungrammatical please raise *their* hand. Then let Lederer and Dowis show you the elegant way out.

❏ *Who/whom* do you think was killed in more movies—Jason or Freddy Krueger? The answer is *who,* not *whom.* But, like it or not, *whom* is still alive in formal prose. Now you can learn to use it correctly.

❏ Is your writing too wordy? Test yourself in *THE WRITE WAY* (and then let's have a discussion on this particular issue some time at a later date).

❏ Is syntax your trouble? Try this recipe: *If your kitten will not drink cold milk, put it in the microwave oven for a few seconds* (but not before Lederer and Dowis show you how to sort out the antecedents).

❏ Orthographically challenged? Discover six handy and painless home remedies that can make you a better speller.

IT'S ALL IN

THE WRITE WAY

The SPELL* Guide to Real-Life Writing

---

*Society for the Preservation of English Language and Literature

THE
WRITE
WAY

The S.P.E.L.L.* Guide
to Real-Life Writing

RICHARD LEDERER
and
RICHARD DOWIS

*Society for the Preservation
of English Language and Literature*

POCKET BOOKS
New York   London   Toronto   Sydney   Tokyo   Singapore

An *Original* Publication of POCKET BOOKS

POCKET BOOKS, a division of Simon & Schuster Inc.
1230 Avenue of the Americas, New York, NY 10020

Library of Congress Cataloging-in-Publication Data

Lederer, Richard, 1938–
    The write way : the S.P.E.L.L.* guide to real-life writing/by
Richard Lederer and Richard Dowis.
        p. cm.
    *Society for the Preservation of English Language and
Literature.
    Includes bibliographical references.
    ISBN 0-671-52670-7
    1. Authorship. I. Dowis, Richard, 1930– . II. Society for
the Preservation of English Language and Literature. III. Title.
    PN145.L335   1995
    808'.02—dc20
                                                            95-17060
                                                            CIP

First Pocket Books trade paperback printing October 1995

10 9 8 7 6 5 4 3 2 1

Cover design by Joanna Reisman

Printed in the U.S.A.

To the men and women of SPELL
and especially to
Mary Louise Gilman,
a great friend to us and a great lady to all who know her

Contents

Introduction

The Write Way grew out of our involvement with SPELL, the Society for the Preservation of English Language and Literature, an international nonprofit organization that promotes high standards of English. The vast majority of SPELL members are neither grammarians nor professional writers. Most are people who simply love language and want to use it well. To each new member, SPELL issues a little handbook that contains, in addition to membership information, a few tips on writing, grammar, usage, and punctuation. Many tell us they have found our tips beneficial, and that is what led us to write this book. We think the book will help you to write better—and to write right. Its approach is *practical*, not theoretical. It offers *answers*, not equivocation. It works equally well as a self-study manual or a quick-reference guidebook. *The Write Way* includes exercises to enable you to gauge your progress or test your knowledge.

We expect the people who read this book to be, like the membership of SPELL, an extraordinarily diverse group. Some write for pleasure, a few for pay; but all share with us a love and respect for the English language, its beauty, variety, and majesty. We hope they also share our belief that language is fun.

Most of the principles of good writing and usage apply to all kinds of writing, so we have made no effort to distinguish among the many types of writing our readers are likely to do. Between us, we have many years of experience as writers and teachers. We draw from this experience for much of the book's content. English is a living language. It grows and changes continually—accepting, rejecting, expanding. A word that means one thing today might mean another tomorrow. What is considered a grammatical error today could be an acceptable idiom tomorrow. We recognize the reality of and the need for change even while deploring the mindless permissiveness that pervades the use of English in our society. We believe that *The Write Way* is *a* right way, but we acknowledge that it may not be the *only way*. It is, as the subtitle says, a guide. It is not a bible.

We had fun writing it. We hope you will have fun using it.

RICHARD LEDERER
Concord, New Hampshire

RICHARD DOWIS
Waleska, Georgia

□ 1 □

What's So Tough About Writing?

Writing is easy. Just put down one word after another and drop in a comma when you want to slow down and a period when you want to stop. Make sure every sentence has a subject and a verb, preferably in that order, and sprinkle in a few adjectives and adverbs just to liven things up.

Well, there might be a *little* more to it than that. The truth is, writing is *not* easy. At least, *good* writing is not. It requires work and thought. It requires knowledge of your subject, an understanding of the mechanics of putting together coherent sentences, and at least a working knowledge of the conventions—let's not call them rules—of grammar, punctuation, and syntax that give order and consistency to the use of our language. Most of all, it requires persistence. Good writing is the result of rewriting, and rewriting can be drudgery. Notice that we have said nothing about inspiration, brilliance, or that mysterious business "creativity"—nice players to have on your team, but not necessary.

There is, in fact, nothing mysterious about writing. Anyone can learn to write better, and in our opinion, everyone ought to. Where do we start? As the song says, "Let's start at the very beginning, a very good place to

1

start." The beginning, we believe, is knowing good writing when you see it.

At one time, tubes of a well-known brand of toothpaste bore these instructions: "For best results, squeeze the tube from the bottom and flatten it as you go up." Is this good writing? Well, it certainly isn't eloquent, but we have to say it is good. It's good because it's simple and direct. It does what it is supposed to do. It says what it needs to say and stops. It has no unnecessary words; nothing can be omitted; nothing need be added. It may be the most ignored advice since the Seventh Commandment, but it makes its point. Besides, it is a suggestion, not a commandment.

Now consider this passage from an article on house organs:

> Today, in an increasingly mobile, tormented, and fragmented society, the role and purpose of a company publication is to build a silhouette of pertinence and to make effective contributions toward moderation across a protean spectrum of a corporation's public. The result is good business!

Is that good writing? The writer obviously was literate, with a good vocabulary and a knowledge of sentence structure. But the passage is meaningless. The writer strove to impress, not to impart any information about company publications. No, it is *not* good writing.

The terms *good* and *bad* are both relative and subjective when applied to writing. We can apply the adjective *bad* with more confidence than *good*. There is a greater degree of consensus as to what makes writing bad, but *good*, like beauty, is in the eye of the beholder. We do, nonetheless, offer some examples of writing that we think is good. They come from a variety of sources. The first is from *Smithsonian* magazine. The article, by Don Stap, describes the ecosystem of some seemingly inhospitable land in Florida. As you read the passage, notice the strong verbs and vivid similes:

> As the fire approached to within 30 feet, it felt like a hot iron pressed against my chest. We began to back up. The palmetto fronds before us crackled and sizzled, disintegrating from the heat even before the flames reached them. Menges gestured to a blackened area behind us. The roar of the fire, like a sheet of metal being whipped back and forth, made conversation nearly impossible. We stepped back into the safety of the burned-out scrub, then backed up further. The 70-foot tidal wave of flame coming at us hit a wall of nothing and fell to the foot of the last oaks. A cactus contorted in the intense heat, slumping like a deflated balloon.

Turning to fiction, we offer a selection from "The Tree of Night," a short story by Truman Capote:

> It was winter. A string of naked bulbs, from which it seemed all warmth had been drained, illuminated the little depot's cold, windy platform. Earlier in the evening it had rained, and now icicles hung along the station-house eaves like some crystal monster's teeth. Except for a girl, the platform was deserted. The girl wore a gray flannel suit, a raincoat, and a plaid scarf. Her hair, parted in the middle and rolled up neatly on the sides, was rich blondish brown; and, while her face tended to be too thin and narrow, she was, though not extraordinarily so, attractive.

From the world of business, here is an excerpt from a tribute to the retiring chairman of Equifax, Inc., published in the corporation's 1988 annual report:

> In the ebb and flow of business, corporate leaders come and go. Most serve with distinction because they are right for their times; but now and then comes one who is right for *all* times, who makes a lasting mark on his company's culture, who sets standards of conduct and performance that are never out of date.
>
> Such a man is W. Lee Burge.

Lee Burge was an 18-year-old student at Georgia State University when he accepted a job in the mail room of Equifax, then known as Retail Credit Company. The year was 1936. From then until he retired on June 30, 1988, he served this company with distinction that was a shining constant during an era of relentless change.

The next section is from *The Lessons of History,* by Will and Ariel Durant:

History is subject to geology. Every day the sea encroaches somewhere upon the land, or the land upon the sea; cities disappear under the water, and cathedrals ring their melancholy bells. Mountains rise and fall in the rhythms of emergence and erosion; rivers swell up and flood, or dry up, or change their course; valleys become deserts, and isthmuses become straits. To this geologic eye all the surface of the earth is a fluid form, and man moves upon it as insecurely as Peter walking on the waves to Christ.

From John Steinbeck's *America and the Americans*:

Kirk dressed in a blue shirt and overalls like most farmers, but he left his orchard only once a week. On Saturday he came to a little feed store my father owned and bought ten cents' worth of middlings—about five pounds, I suppose. Middlings were simply ground wheat with the chaff left in; it would be called whole wheat now, but then it was sold for chicken and pig feed. His weekly purchase was remarkable because the Kirks had neither chickens nor pigs. Mrs. Kirk and her daughter were rarely seen. They never left the orchard, but we could peer through the black cypress hedge which surrounded the orchard and see two gaunt, gray women, so much alike that you couldn't tell which was mother and which was daughter. As far as anyone knew, the ten cents' worth of middlings were all Mr. Kirk ever bought. First the daughter faded and sickened and died, and soon after, Mrs. Kirk went the same way. The coroner said they starved to death; we would call it malnutrition now—but there was no evidence of violence.

People did mind their own business then. But I do know that after they died, Mr. Kirk bought five cents' worth of middlings a week.

Advertising copy is often maligned for being overblown or downright insulting, but the best copywriters, disciplined by the need to pack a lot of product appeal into a little space or time, are capable of good writing. Good advertising slogans, like good writing of any kind, stand the test of time. They are remembered long after they have been discontinued. You probably can easily name the products and companies the following slogans represent:

It's the real thing.

We bring good things to life.

When it rains it pours.

Quality is Job 1.

To prove that you don't have to have a university degree to write effectively, here is a letter to advice-columnist Abigail Van Buren from an elementary school pupil. Notice how the young man uses exact quantities and types of food to make his case. Generalities, such as "We found a lot of sandwiches and other stuff in the garbage can," would have been much less effective:

DEAR ABBY: I am a third grader at Marion Street School in Lynbrook, N.Y. Our teacher, Mr. Freifield, took the class down to the lunchroom to find out how many students threw out their lunches. . . .

First, we found out how many kids ate in the lunch room every day. There were 252. Then we looked in the garbage cans and counted the whole sandwiches that were thrown out. There were 39 untouched sandwiches, still in their wrappers. There were 30 half-eaten sandwiches still unwrapped. Peanut butter and jelly were thrown out the most!

We figured that almost one out of every four people threw away all or half their lunch. With people starving all over the world, that is a lot of food to waste. It was enough to make you sick.

We counted the drinks, too. We found 22 whole containers of drink thrown out. Some were milk, but most were juice.

There was a whole pile of fruit—apples, oranges and bananas—that was thrown into the garbage. Good grapes, too.

Our class decided that maybe the parents should ask their kids what they want for lunch, then maybe the kids wouldn't throw out so much. Thank you.

—Clayton Cohn, N.Y.

Finally, just for the fun of it, we take a leap back more than a century and offer some words uttered by Judge Roy Bean, the famous "law west of the Pecos," in sentencing a murderer to be hanged:

Jose Xaviar Gonzales, in a few short weeks it will be spring, the snows of winter will flee away, the ices will vanish, and the air will become soft and balmy. In short, Jose Xaviar Gonzales, the annual miracle of the years will awaken and come to pass—but you won't be there.

From every tree-top some wild woods songster will carol his mating song, butterflies will sport in the sunshine, the busy bee will hum happy as it pursues its accustomed vocation. The gentle breeze will tease the tassels of wild grasses, and all nature, Jose Xaviar Gonzales, will be glad, but you, you won't be there to enjoy it because I now command the sheriff or some other officers of the county to lead you out to some remote spot, swing you by the neck from a knotting bow of some sturdy oak and let you hang until you are dead.

And so, Jose Xaviar Gonzales, I further command that such officers retire quickly from your dangling corpse, that vultures may descend from the heavens upon your filthy body until nothing shall remain but the bare, bleached bones of a cold-blooded, blood-thirsty, sheep-stealing, murdering son of a bitch.

Now *that*, as teenagers used to say, is telling it like it is.

What do these samples have in common, coming as they do from a wide variety of sources? If they are *good*, what makes them good? Most important, they are simple and direct. Almost anyone can understand them, and they don't contain many unnecessary words. Unlike the passage from the article about house organs, they are unpretentious. They do what their authors intended. As you continue in this book, you will learn other characteristics of good writing. Meanwhile, let's look at a set of basic criteria by which to judge writing.

The Five C's

The Five C's can be an effective way to judge writing. We don't know their origin, but they have been around for a long time in one form or another. They are:

CLEAR

CORRECT

CONCISE

COMPLETE

CONSIDERATE

Good writing is clear. If writing is not clear, it is useless at best. At worst it can cause serious and perhaps costly misunderstanding. Misused words, flawed grammar, poor sentence structure, nonspecific language, redundancy, and verbosity can all cause unclear writing. However, writing can be unclear without any of these faults, as the passage from the article on house organs demonstrates. Conversely, ungrammatical language can be clear. When prize-fight manager Joe Jacobs protested a decision by saying, "We was robbed," he not only spoke understandably, he achieved linguistic immortality.

Good writing is correct. This means it is correct as to its content as well as grammar, spelling, word usage, and punctuation.

Good writing is concise. It does not contain a lot of unnecessary words or information. An anecdote about Abraham Lincoln portrays the gangly Emancipator being ridiculed by a political opponent for his long legs. Mr. Lincoln's response is that his legs are the perfect length—just long enough to reach the floor. That's the way writing ought to be—just long enough to reach . . . whatever.

Good writing is complete. One of life's most frustrating experiences is to read something you're interested in or need to know about and find it lacks pertinent information. When you're writing, stop when, but not until, you've said all you need to say.

Good writing is considerate. It considers the reader's time, intellect, needs, and sensibilities. If writing is verbose or *unnecessarily* long, it wastes the reader's time and is inconsiderate. If it is pompous, it is inconsiderate. If it offends because of intended or unintended racial, religious, or sexist slurs, it is inconsiderate. If it is incomplete, it is inconsiderate. Likewise, if it belabors a point or is more detailed than necessary, it is inconsiderate. The commissioners of St. Johns County, Florida, alarmed about the skimpy costumes worn by the young women employed by a local vendor to sell hotdogs, approved an antinudity statute that included this paragraph:

> The area at the rear of the human body (sometimes known as gluteus maximus) which lies between two imaginary lines running parallel to the ground when a person is standing, the first or top of such lines being one-half inch below the top of the vertical cleavage of the nates (i.e., the prominence formed by the muscles running from the back

of the hip to the back of the leg) and the second or bottom line being one-half inch above the lowest part of the curvature of the fleshy protuberance (sometimes referred to as the gluteal fold), and between two imaginary lines, one on each side of the body (the "outside lines"), which outside lines are perpendicular to the ground and to the horizontal lines described above and which perpendicular lines pass through the outermost point(s) at which each nate meets the outer side of each leg.

The entire paragraph can be expressed as one word—*buttocks. The Random House Dictionary of the English Language* defines *buttocks* quite adequately with twelve words.

A Five C's Checklist

To help you to judge writing, yours or someone else's, we offer the following checklist based on the Five C's:

Is it clear?

☐ Is it punctuated for easy reading and understanding? Does your punctuation follow conventional practices?
☐ Have you used words and phrases likely to be familiar to your reader?
☐ Have you used specific language rather than generalities where specificity is important?
☐ Have you taken into account the reader's likely knowledge of the subject?
☐ Is the material organized logically and efficiently?
☐ Is your writing free of ambiguities, words and phrases that can be interpreted more than one way?

Is it correct?

☐ Have you doubled-checked your information?
☐ Are grammar, spelling, sentence structure, and word choice up to standard?
☐ Have you proofread your work carefully?

Is it concise?

☐ Is it simple and direct, straight to the point?
☐ Is it free of irrelevant or unnecessary details?
☐ Have you used relatively short sentences and paragraphs?
☐ Can you eliminate any words without sacrificing meaning?

Is it complete?

☐ If you were the reader instead of the writer, would you have all the information you needed or wanted on the subject?
☐ Does it answer the basic questions of *who, what, where, when,* and *why,* if those questions are pertinent?

Is it considerate?

☐ Is it written to inform, not to impress?
☐ Is it free of language or implications that might offend your reader?
☐ Is it clear, correct, concise, and complete?

Judging by the Five C's

Printed below are three writing samples with our criticism and suggested revision following each example. Read each one carefully and apply the criteria from the Five C's Checklist. If you feel it does not meet the criteria, revise it. Then read our comments and compare your revision, if any, with ours. The first sample is from a document prepared by a representative of a huge financial institution. It is not a legal document. Its purpose is to help the company's loan committee decide whether to make a loan on an apartment complex:

> The primary risk in this project is the property's failure to lease-up to breakeven occupancy. The risk is mitigated by the high occupancy in the competing projects of 95% and the appropriate mix of apartments of 10 studios, the most difficult to rent with the highest vacancy, to 110 one-bedroom units, to 31 two-bedroom units. The risk is further mitigated by the experience of the borrower team,

which includes The Crossing, a highly respected management team specializing in elderly housing facilities primarily in the west.

Weak or nonexistent punctuation is the main problem with this paragraph. It is also wordy and the sentences are poorly structured. The phrase "specializing in elderly housing facilities" is good for a chuckle because it seems to say that the "borrower team" specializes in slums. Here is our revision:

> The primary risk in this project is that it may not attract enough renters to break even. This risk, however, is mitigated by three factors: (1) competing projects are 95% occupied, (2) the borrower has a respected management team that specializes in housing for the elderly, mostly in the West, and (3) the property has a desirable mix of units—110 one-bedroom units, which are the easiest to rent; 31 two-bedroom units; and only 10 studios, which are the hardest to rent.

Notice how numbering the mitigating factors makes the paragraph easier to handle. Introducing semicolons gives order to the difficult sentence that describes the mix of rental units.

The next example is a one-sentence paragraph from a letter an accounting firm sent to partners (not accountants) in a real estate venture:

> In our opinion, subject to the financial statements of such adjustments, if any, as might have been required had the outcome of the uncertainty about the recoverability and classification of recorded asset amounts and the amounts and classification of liabilities referred to in the preceding paragraph been known, the financial assets referred to in the first paragraph present fairly the assets, liabilities and partners' deficiencies of Green Belt Partners, Ltd., as of December 31, 1987, and its revenues for the year then ended, on the basis of Note 1, which basis has been applied in a manner consistent with that of the preceding year.

We found this difficult to revise because it is almost impossible to understand. Nevertheless, we made an effort to repair it by eliminating much of the wordy detail that kept the paragraph from making sense:

> We believe that the statements referred to in the first paragraph of this letter reflect accurately the financial condition of Green Belt Partners, Ltd., as of December 31, 1987. However, the status of certain recorded assets of the partnership is uncertain, and our opinion is subject to change if any adjustments in the partnership's financial statements should be necessary.

Finally, let's go back to 1942, when the United States was at war and precautions against air raids were a part of everyday life. An aide to President Franklin D. Roosevelt wrote this directive to federal employees:

> Such preparations shall be made as will completely obscure all Federal buildings and non-Federal buildings occupied by the Federal government during an air raid for any period of time from visibility by reason of internal or external illumination.

We didn't have to revise this one, because President Roosevelt had already done it. "Tell them," he instructed his aide, "that in buildings where they have to keep the work going to put something across the windows." We presume that's what the aide did, although we doubt that, in his bureaucratic heart of hearts, he was happy about it.

POINTS TO PONDER AND REMEMBER

- ☛ There is no good writing, only good rewriting.
- ☛ The best writing is simple and direct, easily understood by people for whom it is intended.
- ☛ Good writing is considerate of the reader's time, intellect, needs, and sensibilities.

□ 2 □

Getting It Started,
Keeping It Going

"Writing is easy," said the late novelist Gene Fowler. "All you have to do is stare at a blank sheet of paper until drops of blood form on your forehead." You're more likely to stare at a blank computer screen, but the agony you feel is the same as Fowler's, and the blood on your forehead is the same low-tech red.

The affliction is called "writer's block." It comes at that terrible time when a term paper is due and you haven't written a line, when the boss expects to see your memo first thing tomorrow morning, when you need to write a letter to your senator telling why you favor some particular legislation. You just can't get started. Your brain seems to have turned to mush. You can't find words to express the simplest idea—if you even have an idea to express. The flood of thoughts you had before drifting off to sleep last night has dried to a trickle.

When you're in the grip of writer's block, you experience the call of nature more often, you have an unusual craving for coffee, you cannot stand the thought of an unsharpened pencil in the house, and you remember things you meant to do—important things, like rearranging your sock drawer or waxing the shell of your pet turtle. You'll do anything to put off the time when you have to write that first sentence.

You may derive some small comfort from the knowledge that it happens to all of us now and then. Even professional writers sometimes wish they had taken up something easy, like brain surgery or determining the sex of baby chickens. But knowing that others have the problem doesn't tell you what to do about it.

A diagnosis of the malady might help. You may be surprised to know that writer's block is most often an organizational problem. When you sit down to write, you probably know what you want to say. In fact, your mental circuits might be overloaded with information: The more you have in mind to say, the harder it is to say anything. That's because you don't know what should come first. If you have only one simple thing to say, there's no problem. If you have two things to say, it's decision time.

Professionals who work on strict deadlines—journalists, for example—are trained to write fast. They couldn't meet their deadlines if they had to agonize over how to start every article. They use some techniques that you might find helpful. In this chapter, we will discuss these techniques and give you other tips for getting your project started and keeping it going. Not all of them will work for you. Not all of them work for us. Different writers, different methods; different material, different organization.

Trite but True

An ancient Chinese proverb tells us that "A journey of a thousand miles begins with a single step." And one common piece of advice for writers that is offered in most books on writing and by most teachers of writing is "Start with an outline." Both are trite but true.

When you contemplate a journey, you may know where you want to go, what you want to do when you get there, and some of what to expect along the way, but until you plot your course on a map, you can't be certain of the best route. An outline is the writer's map.

The process of making an outline forces you to think logically about what you want to say. Once the outline is complete, it gives you confidence that you know where you're going with your writing and how you will get there. In other words, it keeps you on track. You don't have to follow it exactly, but even when you depart from it, you'll be doing so purposefully and you can return to the outline at any time.

Even short items are easier to write if you take time, before you begin writing, to jot down a few points you want to make. Arranged in logical order, these points constitute an outline.

An outline need not be—should not be—too detailed or too elaborate. Nor should it be set in concrete. Don't worry about whether your outline follows some standard form. If you become too engrossed in making the outline, you might come down with "outline block," which may be worse than writer's block. When this happens, the outline has become the problem rather than the solution.

Some teachers stress the outline form and may even require their students to submit their outlines for approval before beginning to write. This seems to be the equivalent of judging sculpture by the quality of the sculptor's tools. If a student's final written product is good, the outline is irrelevant. If the writing is bad, however, a teacher might suspect that the student has not learned the value of making an outline and may then be justified in asking to see an outline for future assignments.

How to Outline

If we could sit beside you and guide you through your next writing project, we would begin by asking you a question about the subject. Your answer would stimulate another question, then another and another until we had picked your brain of all you knew about the subject. Then we would help you group related items together and arrange the groups in some kind of logical order. You might write the information on index cards for easy arranging, as students often do when they research a subject in the library. One writer we know types items of information at random, then cuts the pages into strips, one item per strip, and arranges the strips in order.

For some kinds of writing, the best arrangement would be chronological. For others it would be to place the most important things first; for still others, to move from the general to the specific. If you organize your items of information well, the results can be dramatic. When the arranging is complete, you will find the mush has gone from your brain and your craving for coffee has abated. Your forehead has stopped bleeding, and you won't need a transfusion after all. Now you're ready to write. In fact, you may find that much of your writing has already been done.

Some computer programs designed to help you prepare to write are based on this question-and-answer method. The computer's questions, however, are often too general to be useful. The more specific your questions and answers, the better your outline will be. Still, some generalities may be necessary. For example, ask yourself:

Why am I writing?

Who are my readers?

What effect do I want my writing to have on the readers?

What is the main idea I want to get across?

What are the major supporting facts?

What are the minor supporting facts?

These general questions probably should precede the specific questions. Keep their answers in mind as you develop the specifics.

The Five W's

In the late nineteenth century, a journalism textbook introduced a concept that even today is known to every newspaper reporter and is still taught in schools of journalism. It is called the Five W's—*who, what, when, where,* and *why.* The point of the Five W's is that all information a reporter might need could be reduced to the answers to those five questions. Some modern instructors throw in an *H,* for *how,* but some people put catsup on scrambled eggs. The Five W's are supposed to remind reporters of the information to be included in the "lead," the first two or three paragraphs of a news story.

Generations of journalists—cubs and veterans—have used the Five W's as both a starter and a reminder. You can use them for the same purposes when you write memos, letters, reports, and other communications. Some of the questions implied by the Five W's might be:

WHO will read this communication?

WHO will be affected by it?

WHO are the main people involved?

WHAT is my purpose in writing?

WHAT do I want to tell my readers?

WHAT do I want them to do?

WHEN did or will the action or event take place?

WHEN do I expect my readers to react?

WHERE did or will the event or activity take place?

WHERE can the reader obtain more information if it is needed?

WHY do the readers need the information?

WHY is this the best way to provide them with the information?

The Five W's are a good way to test your writing for completeness.

The Inverted Pyramid

Another useful journalistic technique is an organizational pattern known as the "inverted pyramid." The traditional way to tell a story is to lead the reader through a series of facts to the climax or main point. The inverted pyramid does the opposite. It starts with the main point and ends with the least important. All items of information in between appear in descending order of importance. By the time you reach the end of the article, you're into "throwaway" information. This is like starting a joke with the punch line or a "whodunit" with who did it.

The inverted pyramid makes reading a newspaper article more efficient. The reader can get the essential facts by zipping through the first few paragraphs. Readers who want more details can stick with the story until it tails off into nothing. The inverted pyramid, however, probably was not developed with the reader in mind. Most likely it evolved as a solution to the problem of copy fitting—making an article fit the space allotted to it. When newspapers were printed from metal type, everything had to fit perfectly for the page form to "lock up." If a story, after being set in type, was a few lines too long for its "hole," someone had to decide how to cut it. If the story was written in the inverted pyramid style, a printer could safely lop off a few lines from the end without fear of doing violence to the story. If a story had to be cut from the middle, an editor or the reporter would have to do it. The copy would then have to go back to the linotype machine for expensive and time-consuming resetting.

Regardless of its origin, the inverted pyramid survives in modern journalism. In modified form, it can be useful to both the writer and the reader in certain kinds of communications, particularly business letters and memoranda. Like busy newspaper readers, busy memo readers can get the essential facts quickly and, if necessary, can read the full document for details. In this sense, the first two or three paragraphs of a business communication may serve the same purpose that an "executive summary" serves in a long document that includes many details that are important to some, but not all, of the people who read it.

List It

When you have to write a piece that discusses several items, consider presenting some of the material in list form rather than narrative. For example, if you're reporting on a meeting in which several topics were discussed, you might handle it something like this:

At the board meeting, directors discussed the following:

—proposed acquisition of Acme Widget, Inc.;

—appointment of a new auditing firm;

—appointment of Elizabeth Morgenstern as executive vice president;

—closing of the company's Mississippi plant;

—purchase of a new mainframe computer for the home office; and,

—purchase of copies of *The Write Way* to distribute to all management personnel.

Each item could then be discussed individually with several sentences or even paragraphs devoted to it. This is a much more efficient way to present a great deal of material than to write it all in narrative form. The reader can glance at the list, take in the essential points, and decide which items require closer examination. Material of this type in narrative could make difficult writing and tedious reading, especially if the writer felt the need to introduce each new subject with a connective such as "Another item on the agenda was . . ."

In listing information, try to keep all items on the list in the same grammatical form. For example, in the list above, you should not toss in something like "President Hofnagle proposed that Elizabeth Morgenstern be promoted to executive vice president." That would be out of sync with the other items and would not go with "At the board meeting, directors discussed the following."

Think First Draft

Another common cause of writer's block is lack of confidence. If you are concerned that what you write won't "sound good" or do what you want it to do, you may be reluctant to start writing until you gain confidence that you know exactly what you want to say and exactly how you want to say it. Even after you've made a start, lack of confidence may slow you down. You can overcome this difficulty easily by reminding yourself of two things: first, this is the first draft; no one will see it except me; second, there is no good writing, only good rewriting.

As you write, continue to think first draft. So what if it's not perfect? So what if you opened with Fact A when Fact B might be more important? So what if you have put an extra *f* in *Hofnagle*? He won't read the first draft. If you're not sure how to spell *Hofnagle*, circle it or underline it to remind yourself to check it out before the final draft.

For some writers, the first draft is so rough that it is little more than an outline. Whether you make yours that rough may depend on your style, your work habits, the nature of the writing project, or how much time you have to complete the project. Very few writers are satisfied with their first drafts. You shouldn't be.

In writing the first draft, start anywhere. The idea is to begin to put flesh on the bones—your outline—but not to strive for perfection. Get it down in chronological order if that's the easiest way. Or start at what might seem to be the end and work back. Momentum is the important thing. When you have it, don't let it go. If you lack a fact or figure, don't stop to look it up; leave a blank and fill it in later. If a word you have chosen doesn't seem to fit, use it anyway. The thesaurus will still be on the shelf when you're working on the final draft.

If you're working on a long document, one you can't complete in a single sitting, here's a way to "jump-start" your writing engine when you return from your hiatus: Go back several paragraphs, or even several pages, and copy what you have already written. You'll find that by the time you reach the point where you stopped, your mind is back in gear and you're off and running again. Some writers purposely stop writing in mid-sentence because completing the sentence helps them to start their next session.

Finally, if the malady lingers, if you get stuck and feel that you can't write another word, get up and take a walk, listen to music, jog around the block, take a nap—anything to clear your conscious mind of the problem and let your unconscious mind take over. This can work miracles.

Buckle Down; Get Serious

Face it. The time will come when you will be writing the final draft. It may be the second, third, or fourth, but it is the final. This is the draft that others will see. Now is the time to polish your language to a high gloss, to double-check your facts, to make certain that spelling, grammar, and punctuation are beyond reproach. This is when you make those organizational adjustments that change the document from a collection of facts to a coherent, persuasive piece of writing that will accomplish what you want it to accomplish.

If possible, allow some time between your next-to-last draft and your final draft. This will help you to view the project with a fresh perspective. And after you have completed the final draft, let someone else look it over. The worse proofreader is the person who wrote the material. That's because the writer often sees what is supposed to be there rather than what's actually there.

Word processing has made revising easy. No longer do you have to imagine how a word, a sentence, or a paragraph would fit in another location. With a few clicks of the mouse, you can see for yourself. And if you don't like what you see, you can move the paragraph back just as easily. No longer do you have to search through your document line by line to see if you have corrected the spelling of *Hofnagle* everywhere you used the name. You can use the find-and-replace command to do it for you. Grammar checkers can warn you of some writing faults, and spelling checkers help you catch spelling and typographical errors, although they cannot distinguish between words that sound alike but have different spellings and meanings (see Chapter 10).

No technology, however remarkable, can turn bad writing into good. Only you can do that. You have to work at it. We've said it before: There is no good writing, only good rewriting. Believe it.

Points to Ponder and Remember

- ☛ Writer's block isn't fatal; it just seems so at times.
- ☛ Giving your unconscious mind a chance can work miracles.
- ☛ When you have momentum, keep it going.

□ 3 □

Target Your Writing

During the planning and writing of this book, we kept the telephone lines humming between Concord, New Hampshire, and Waleska, Georgia. Did your ears burn? They should have. Many of our conversations were about you. Yes, *you*. Our reader. We asked ourselves a lot of questions about you. Why would you want to buy a book on writing? Do you write regularly in your work, or do you write only now and then? What aspects of writing and usage would help you most? Would you respond better to an informal or formal style? Do you enjoy language?

Of course, we know that Reader A is not Reader B. Everyone who buys this book is an individual with individual needs and preferences, and we could never hope to satisfy all of them in all ways. Nevertheless, after considering these and other questions, we concluded that:

a. The title of our book, *The Write Way,* and the subtitle, which includes the word *Guide,* would appeal to people looking for answers to perplexing problems in writing and usage.
b. Although our readers were likely to be intelligent and educated, they probably would not be interested in highly technical or pedantic discussions.

c. People who want to improve their writing want an indication of their progress; hence, the book should contain exercises and quizzes.

d. Our readers would prefer a relaxed, informal style and would enjoy humor and light touches in our illustrations.

These and other conclusions helped shape *The Write Way*. They helped us to target our writing to the people we expected to buy and use the book. Knowing who your readers are and what they want is surely the first, and perhaps the most important, step in writing.

A line from an old joke goes, "Have I reached the party with whom I am speaking?" When you write a letter, a memorandum, or some other communication, you can't stop in the middle and ask, "Are you with me? Have I reached the party to whom I am writing?" If you've waited that long to ask, you probably haven't. Before you write, you must decide how you can target the communication to your audience. It is not always easy to do. The language you use, the tone you adopt, the degree of formality or informality in your style—these are some of the factors that affect the way your readers respond to what you write.

Informality: How much?

We are living in an age of informality. Gone, thank heavens, are the days when almost all written matter, even letters between friends or relatives, was stiff and formal. This does not mean, however, that informality is always appropriate. Different kinds of writing, different subjects, and different audiences call for different degrees of informality.

We consciously decided to adopt an informal style for this book. We achieve this by using contractions and personal pronouns freely. We refer to our readers as *you* and to ourselves as *we*. We think this style is right for our subject and audience. It's appropriate for *you* because we know you. We have met you—in seminars we've conducted and classes we've taught. You've been in audiences we've addressed, and we've even exchanged letters with you.

No one can decide for you what degree of formality or informality is appropriate for your audience when you write. No rule applies except the "rule" of common sense.

Seek a Common Ground

The chairman of a Fortune 500 company kept prominently displayed in his office a picture of an attractive family group—a man and woman who appeared to be in their seventies; a younger woman, about the age of the executive, holding an infant; and a couple of handsome teenagers. In the foreground sat a golden retriever who looked as if to say, "These are my people and I'm proud of them." Visitors to the chairman's office often remarked on the photograph, usually complimenting him on his "fine family." Most of the time, he just smiled and thanked the visitor. Once, however, a visitor pursued the subject and asked if the older couple were his parents.

"No," the executive replied. "In fact, I don't even know their names." Then he explained to the puzzled visitor that he had hired a commercial photographer to make the picture and that all the people in it were professional models.

"I keep the picture for a very special purpose," the chairman said. "I write many letters—to shareholders, employees, customers, and suppliers. I rarely know the person I write to, so I just pick one of the people in the picture and pretend I'm writing to that person. That way, I feel as if I'm writing to a human being, not just a name. It helps me get some warmth and feeling in my letter. Business letters can be awfully cold. I guess I've written to everyone in the picture hundreds of times—except the dog, and I'd write to him if I had a good reason."

Good yarn. It probably isn't true, but that's not important. What is important is the sentiment behind it. Here was a busy executive, sensitive enough to the possible effects of his letters to take time to seek a common ground, or a bond, with the people to whom he wrote. The common ground he sought was the best of all—simple humanity.

Good speakers almost always begin their speeches by establishing a common ground with their audiences. They know it will help them get their messages across. A corporate executive from Atlanta was speaking to a group of businesspeople in Chicago. After the obligatory introductory remarks, she said, "As you know, I'm from Atlanta, and down in Atlanta we call Chicago the *other* city that works."

The laughter and applause told her she had hit the mark. The humor brought her and her audience together, for people who share laughter share something priceless. To strengthen the bond, she went on to point out the things Atlanta and Chicago have in common and implied that Atlantans, like Chicagoans, were proud of their city.

When presidents of the United States address the nation, they usually open with "My fellow Americans." They're saying, "I'm one of you. I happen to be president, but I'm an American just as you are and I'm proud of it. I'm just as concerned as you are about the problems we, as Americans, face." Franklin D. Roosevelt used the cozy term *fireside chats* to describe his radio addresses to the nation. Jimmy Carter liked to wear a sweater instead of a coat and tie for some of his television appearances. Ronald Reagan was a master of self-deprecating humor. These were all different ways these presidents had of seeking common ground with their audiences.

Compare the following two possible openings for a business letter and decide which does a better job of establishing a common ground with its audiences.

Compare the following two possible openings for a business letter and decide which does a better job of establishing a common ground:

> Dear Bob:
>
> I enjoyed seeing you during our meeting in Phoenix last week. I'm writing this letter to bring you up to date on some things that have taken place since then.

> Dear Bob:
>
> What a great meeting we had in Phoenix last week! You and your staff really had it organized, and I'm sure everyone benefited from it as much as I did. Since the meeting, some interesting things have happened. Let me tell you about them.

No contest. The second opener is more relaxed. The writer's enthusiasm comes through, and Bob and his staff get a well-deserved compliment for putting on a good meeting. These help establish a bond between Bob and the writer.

When members of the same profession communicate with each other, their common ground might be the language, or jargon, of that profession. When a member of one profession communicates with someone outside the profession, language can prevent their finding a common ground. That is why we caution against overuse of jargon. In a later chapter, we will discuss jargon and its effect on writing.

We would expect an attorney, when writing an article for a law journal, to use legal terms, including the Latin phrases that pervade the argot of the law. Using such terms in an article on the same subject for a business publication might prevent the lawyer from bonding with the audience.

In the opening chapter of this book, we cited as an example of writing that did not meet the test of the Five C's a one-sentence paragraph from a letter an accounting firm sent to members of a real estate partnership. We repeat it here to make another point:

> In our opinion, subject to the financial statements of such adjustments, if any, as might have been required had the outcome of the uncertainty about the recoverability and classification of recorded asset amounts and the amounts and classification of liabilities referred to in the preceding paragraph been known, the financial assets referred to in the first paragraph present fairly the assets, liabilities and partners' deficiencies of Greenbelt Partners, Ltd., as of December 31, 1987, and its revenues for the year then ended, on the basis of Note 1, which basis has been applied in a manner consistent with that of the preceding year.

The writer of this passage made no attempt to meet readers on a common ground. The words themselves aren't the problem; every word is familiar to any literate person. But the way the words are used makes them seem foreign to any reader not familiar with "financespeak." The seemingly endless sentence, the stilted phrases, and the frequent references to other documents and other sections of the letter combine to create a chasm between writer and reader.

Compare the accountant's letter with this excerpt from an article in *Engineering News Record*:

> The wind tunnel analysis developed by Rowen Williams Davies Irvin, Inc., Guelph, Ontario, involved 36 different wind directions. It showed that the maximum east-west base overturning moments are caused by wind blowing along north-south alignment.
>
> The core shear walls in the tower's lower floors handle much of the lateral loading with shear-frame interaction. There are four main shear walls—two I shapes and two C shapes—on a typical floor. These interact with the perime-

ter columns and perimeter spandrel beams through girders
that span from the core to the perimeter.

The article was intended for engineers, and the technical terms are part of the bond between the writer and the
reader. The quality of the writing is markedly superior to
the quality of the writing in the accountant's letter. Although we're not engineers, we have the feeling that we
understand the excerpt from the magazine—or we would
understand it if we understood "core shear walls," "shear-
frame interaction," and "spandrel beams," all engineering terms.

Some professionals, especially attorneys and accountants, will tell you that the need for "legal precision" prevents them from writing in clear, simple language. Don't
believe it. Truth be told, legalese is a way of intimidating
those untrained in the law. It works, too. We venture a
guess that even some judges and lawyers find legalese
bewildering. Yet many attorneys and accountants do succeed in writing simply and concisely.

Simple language can be precise. In 1973, Citibank began
to study customer complaints. Citibank was then the third-
largest suer of consumers in New York City. The bank relied heavily on lawsuits to collect delinquent loans. A task
force appointed by the chairman recommended that the
bank's promissory note be simplified in substance, language, and design. This was accomplished after much
work. The results were striking: The original was two
threatening, legal-size pages of small type that gave meaning to the oft-stated warning "Be sure to read the fine
print." The revision was a single page of larger type, with
paragraphs broken by numbers and subheadings.

In the original, this paragraph "explained" the default
provisions of the note:

In the event of default in the payment of this or any other
Obligation or the performance or observance of any term

or covenant contained herein or in any note or other contract or agreement evidencing or relating to any Obligation or any Collateral on the Borrowor's part to be performed or observed; or that the undersigned Borrowor shall die; or any of the undersigned become insolvent or make an assignment for the benefit of creditors; or a petition shall be filed by or against any of the undersigned under any provision of the Bankruptcy Act; or any money, securities or properties of the undersigned now or hereafter on deposit with or in the possession or under the control of the Bank shall be attached or become subject to distraint proceedings or any order of process of any court; or the bank shall deem itself to be insecure. . . . [and on, and on, and on].

In the simplified note, the passage appeared this way:

I'll be in default:
  1. If I don't pay an installment on time; or
  2. If any other creditor tries by legal process to take any money of mine in your possession.

Citibank adopted new collection procedures along with the simplified note, and within a few years the bank's lawsuits against consumers dropped considerably.

Adult to Adult

The president of a large company wrote a memorandum to employees on the subject of telephone courtesy. Now, telephone courtesy is a subject worthy of executive attention because it affects a company's image. But this memo sounded as if it came from a father scolding his children.

A sales letter from a small lawn-care company claimed that the company "deserved" more business because "the big boys" made it tough for "the little guy" to make a living.

The scolding of the company president and the whining of the small-business owner bring to mind a once popular psychological concept known as transactional analysis (TA). This concept was advanced in the 1950s by psychiatrist Eric Berne and introduced in his book *Games People Play.* A decade or so later, Dr. Thomas A. Harris, a protégé of Dr. Berne, came out with another book on the subject, *I'm O.K.—You're O.K.*

The theory behind TA is that the human personality comprises three discrete elements (behavioral states) called "child," "parent," and "adult." At any given time, one of the three might be dominant in a person. Any "transaction," which is to say any contact between individuals, will be affected by whichever personality element is dominant in each person at the time. A transaction can be a written contact as well as a face-to-face contact.

To understand the three behavioral states, compare these three sentences:

a. If the people in the office weren't so noisy, I could get my work done without having to stay late every day.

b. If you would just plan your work a little better, you could get your work done on time and wouldn't have to stay late every day.

c. When there's a distraction in the hall, I just close my office door so I won't be disturbed.

No doubt you have discerned that the "child" was the dominant personality of the person who wrote the first sentence. Its tone, like that of the business owner's letter, is whiny. The writer makes excuses for failing to complete the work on time and seeks sympathy for having to work late every day.

The second sentence has the I-told-you-so tone that one might use with an errant child—a tone much like that of the telephone-courtesy memo. The "parent" is clearly dominant.

The third sentence sounds very adult. It blames no one. It makes no excuses. It suggests a reasonable solution to the problem.

Applying transactional analysis to writing, we often see examples in which either the "parent" or the "child" dominated the writer. We prefer writing in which the "adult" dominates. No one likes to hear another person whine, make excuses, or blame others. No one likes to be scolded, lectured to, or treated like a six-year-old. Most people respond to reasonable, straightforward communications. Keeping these thoughts in mind as you write will help you to adopt an adult-to-adult tone, which is another way to target your writing toward your readers.

Readability by the Numbers

Attempts have been made over the years to devise a system for measuring readability. A look at two such systems and how they arrive at their conclusions might be interesting and, to the extent that they provide insight into what makes writing work, instructive. The best known (possibly the first) readability measurement system was the brainchild of the late Robert Gunning, a writing consultant. If nothing else, it had a catchy name, the Fog Index, which has become almost a generic term for any system that purports to measure readability. Gunning introduced the Fog Index in the 1950s, though he claimed that it was based on research conducted decades earlier.

The premise of the Fog Index is that readability depends on two factors—sentence length and word length. Although the premise seems a bit simplistic, there is no doubt that short words and sentences make easier reading. Theodore Bernstein, the late assistant managing editor of the *New York Times* and author of several excellent books on usage, advocated one-idea sentences. Thus, Bernstein seems to confirm Gunning's thesis, at least to the extent that one-idea sentences are shorter sentences.

Here are Gunning's instructions for applying the Fog Index:

1. Find the average number of words per sentence. Use a sample of at least 100 words. Divide the total number of words by the number of sentences. This gives you the average sentence length.

2. Count the number of words of three syllables or more per 100 words. Don't count: (a) words that are capitalized; (b) combinations of short, easy words—like *bookkeeper*, (c) verbs that are made three syllables by adding *ed* or *es*—like *created* or *trespasses*.

3. Add the two figures above and multiply by 0.4. This will give you the Fog Index. It corresponds roughly with the number of years of schooling a person must have to read a passage with ease and understanding.

In the late 1950s, Rudolph Flesch, a teacher, attorney, and author of several books on writing, introduced his own system for measuring readability. Dr. Flesch's system is a bit more difficult to apply than Gunning's. It measures readability not in terms of the years of education required to understand a given passage but on a scale of subjective criteria from "formal" to "very popular."

From Flesch's book *A New Way to Better English*, here are instructions for applying his readability yardstick:

To test your writing, count off exactly 100 words as a sample.

You'll run into a few questions as to what is a word. As a rule of thumb, count everything as a word that has white space on either side. Therefore, count the article *a* as a word, and the letter *a* in enumerations, and all numbers, abbreviations, etc. (Examples: *1958*, *G.O.P.*, *½*, *Ph.D.*, *e.g.*) If an abbreviation point falls in the middle of a word, count it as one word, not two. Also count as one word contractions and hyphenated words, for instance, *don't*, *I've*, *half-baked*, *pseudo-science*. Now you are ready for the test count. Start again at the beginning and count one point for each of the following items:

1. Any word with a capital letter in it.
2. Any word that is italicized.

3. All numbers (unless spelled out).
4. All punctuation marks such as commas, hyphens, and abbreviation points. (Periods, colons, semicolons, question marks, exclamation points, quotation marks, parentheses, brackets, apostrophes, etc.)
5. All symbols, such as £, $, ¢, %, &.
6. One extra point for the beginning and ending of a paragraph.

If you have taken a 100-word sample, the sum total of your points is your score. If you have taken several 100-word samples, add up the points in all the samples and divide by the number of samples. The result is your average score for the whole piece of writing. . . .

Your score is likely to be somewhere between 10 and 50. Here is what it means:

Up to 20	Formal
21 to 25	Informal
26 to 30	Fairly popular
31 to 35	Popular
Over 35	Very popular

"Formal" writing, according to Flesch, is found in academic and scientific journals, "informal" in quality magazines such as *Harper's*, "fairly popular" in mass-circulation fiction and nonfiction magazines, and "very popular" in mass-circulation fiction magazines.

We applied the Gunning and Flesch systems to some writing samples. The first is from *Economics Explained*, by Robert Heilbroner and Lester Thurow:

Taken together, the shift to services, the fall in mining output, and the sag in construction account for one third of our total drop in productivity over the past few decades. Thus there are obviously other industries and other reasons behind the productivity problem. Here we are going to zero in on one and only one of these additional explanations. It is the failure of American industry to invest in enough modern capital equipment to stay abreast of its Western partners. Capital equipment alone is certainly not the secret of productivity, but it is a very important part of the problem, as we shall see.

This brings us back, initially, to cars and steel. Why did these industries fare so badly vis-à-vis their international competitors? One reason is simply the failure of American management to make correct decisions. The steel industry decided not to go into oxygenation and continuous casting, and the auto industry decided not to abandon the big car. Both decisions were terribly wrong, particularly because our international competition decided otherwise.

The result is that in 1980, for the first time, Japan actually produced more cars than did the United States (5.5 million against 4.5 million), and Toyota and Nissan have replaced Ford as GM's first ranking competitors. Meanwhile, the following chart shows that the United States has trailed the entire world in converting its steel plants into continuous casting, while foreign companies have ploughed their earnings back into steel.

Following Flesch's instructions, we count 259 words in the passage, which is 2.59 "samples." It scores 37 points, or 14.3 points per sample. That puts it in the "formal" category (academic and scientific journals).

The passage contains thirteen sentences—average length, 19.9 words. It has 16.2 three-syllable words per hundred. Applying the Fog Index formula, we come up with 14.4. This, according to Gunning, means that a person would have to have completed 14.4 years of schooling to read and understand the passage. That is about midway to a bachelor's degree.

Our guess is that Flesch's "formal" equates to 14 or 15 on the Fog Index scale. If so, the Heilbroner-Thurow passage rates about the same with both systems.

The next sample to which we applied the Flesch and Gunning systems comes from Beryl Markham's luminous book, *West with the Night*:

No matter how elaborate the safari on which Makula is engaged as a tracker, he goes about naked from the waist up carrying a full quiver of poisoned arrows. He has seen the work of the best rifles white men have yet produced, but when Makula's nostrils distend after either a good shot or a bad shot, it is not the smell of gunpowder that distends them; it is a kind of restrained contempt for the noisy and unwieldy piece of machinery with its devilish tendency to knock the untutored huntsman flat on his buttocks every time he pulls the trigger.

Safaris come and safaris go, but Makula goes on forever. I suspect at times that he is one of the wisest men I have ever known—so wise that, realizing the scarcity of wisdom, he has never cast a scrap of it away, although I still remember a remark he made to an overzealous newcomer to his profession: "White men pay for danger—we poor ones cannot afford it. Find your elephant, then vanish, so that you may live to find another."

Makula always vanished. He went ahead in the bush with the silence of a shade, missing nothing, and the moment he had brought hunters in sight of the elephant, he disappeared with the silence of a shade, missing everything.

This is a fine piece of writing, especially the last paragraph. The passage has 228 words and scores 11.4, or "formal," by the Flesch method. On the Fog Index, it scores 15.4, which means a first-quarter senior in college could read and understand it. Again, Flesch and Gunning are remarkably close to consensus. Under both systems, the Markham sample shows up as slightly more difficult than the Heilbroner-Thurow sample. The Markham piece has longer sentences, but the economics piece has more three-syllable words.

Next, we offer an excerpt from humorist Dave Barry's book *Bad Habits*:

Okay! Today you begin the physical-fitness program that's going to make you healthy and attractive, like the people in cigarette ads. Step one is to take your pulse, because a healthy heart is the key to physical fitness. The best way to understand why is to examine an actual heart.

You cannot, of course, examine your own, unless you have a high threshold for pain. So trot down to the grocery and ask the butcher for surplus hearts from an assortment of animals—a cow, a pig, a fish, an earthworm. Most butchers will give you the hearts for free, just to get rid of you.

Now take your hearts home, spread them out on a clean, level surface, such as a Ping-Pong table, and examine them. You'll notice the hearts differ in size, but they have one important thing in common: *the animals they were removed from are all dead.*This tells us that hearts are extremely important for physical fitness. Next place your hearts in plastic containers and store them in your freezer in case your children ever need them for science projects.

Now you're ready to take your pulse. The traditional method is to press your fingertips against the artery in your wrist.

The Fog Index indicates that this passage could be understood by a college freshman. According to Flesch, it falls into the "popular" range.

Are readability systems dependable? Will they help you to target your writing to your readers? The answer to both questions is a qualified yes. They are research-based, which gives them some validity. But readability depends on many factors besides the ones these systems rely on most heavily. Still, their essential message cannot be faulted: Shorter words, shorter sentences, shorter paragraphs, and better punctuation do help make writing readable. None of these, however, invariably results in good or even well-targeted writing.

Many of the best computer word-processing programs will test your writing by the Fog Index or other readability systems. This saves all the counting and makes the concept more appealing. By all means, test a sample of your writing now and then. It can't hurt, and it could help.

What you won't find in your word-processing software are these pieces of good advice from the old masters Gunning and Flesch. Here is Gunning's:

Writing is too closely linked to life to be encased in a system. No one can say for sure what writing will succeed. You can't make rules about writing, because rules are a substitute for thought—and you can't write without thinking. Therefore, don't try to write by formula alone. . . . The way to write clearly is to apply principles, not rules, of clear statement.

Here is Flesch's:

[T]here is one more rule—a rule that's probably more important than all the others: *Don't take any of these rules too seriously.* Don't try to write mechanically to fill a set quota of capitals, periods, or quotation marks. . . . Don't strain every nerve to be relaxed and informal.

And here is ours: *Before* you start to write, think about your readers—who they are and what you want them to do or think or feel as a result of what you will write. Ask yourself how much or how little they know about the subject. Decide on the appropriate tone for your writing. Ask what common ground exists between you and them. *After* you've written, read what you've written and try to see it through your reader's eyes. Ask yourself: Have I included the right amount of information? Have I written an adult-to-adult communication? Has what I've written helped form a bond between the reader and me? Does my writing meet the criteria of the Five C's?

POINTS TO PONDER AND REMEMBER

- ☛ The first rule of writing is to know your reader.
- ☛ Simple humanity may be the best bond between writer and reader.
- ☛ Targeting your writing to your reader helps to satisfy at least one of the Five C's—*considerate.*
- ☛ Systems that purport to measure readability may be useful, but they are not infallible.

□ 4 □

Slim Down, Shape Up

Writing today often has too much fat, too little muscle—bulk without strength. Much of what we read these days ranges from slightly flabby to grossly obese. As children, we wrote sentences like "See Dick run." As adults, we're more likely to write, "It is imperative that we carefully observe Richard as he engages in the physical activity of using personal means to transverse the terrain at an accelerated rate of speed."

Exaggerated, you say? Of course; but consider how a state of Georgia transportation study described something called the gravity model, a procedure for estimating the "distribution" of automobile trips:

> This model assumes that the trips produced in a traffic zone are attracted to other traffic zones in direct proportion to the total attractions in the other traffic zones and indirectly proportional to the distance between the traffic zones.

Translation? One guess is as good as another. Here is ours: If traffic is heavy on a given route, many drivers will try a different route if there is one that's not too far away.

Want more? Digest, if you can, this excerpt from a report that a management consultant sent to a client:

> There are some sound and logical reasons for the integra-
> tion of all business efforts throughout the organization (as
> it exists today) or complete segmentation (as it was prac-
> ticed years ago). The next level of abstraction is neither
> integration nor segmentation *but* creating a series of inter-
> dependencies through practical incentive and communica-
> tion techniques while still having differentiation . . . thus
> the potential for the improved focus of managerial, techni-
> cal and support personnel's energies and resources to
> achieve desired results.

These are real, and they are not unusual. Our files bulge
with similar examples from business, government, medicine, education, the arts, science, and technology.

What happens to people's writing in the years between
childhood and maturity? For one thing, *their reasons for
writing change*. The child writes for the best of reasons—
to tell somebody something that is worth telling. Little
Jane Smith wants her friends to know about her dog, Spot.
Her only concern is that her friends know that Spot is "the
bestest dog in the whole wide world." The adult may have
any number of reasons for writing. Mr. Smith, Jane's dad,
also has something worthwhile to write about—his company's new marketing plan, which may or may not be the
"bestest" marketing plan in the industry. But his real reason for writing a long memo about the plan is that he
wants to be perceived as having had "input" into the plan's
development. As he writes, he worries about the impression his writing might make on his colleagues, especially
his boss. He chooses his words carefully—the more, and
the longer, the better. Even if his instinct tells him to write
simply, he's afraid to, lest his memo not be taken seriously.

Jane has no such fear. When she writes, she uses simple,
clear, unaffected, second-grade vocabulary; Mr. Smith
draws on marketing terms he learned while earning his
M.B.A. He relies heavily on the jargon of his business. For
good measure, he might throw in a *quid pro quo*, a *sine*

qua non, a couple of viable alternatives, and a new set of parameters. When it's done, he has produced a bloated, tedious, pompous piece of writing that is, like the example from the transportation study, almost incomprehensible. We can be sure it lacks the warmth, sincerity, and directness that are characteristics of most good writing.

As Jane grows older, her writing gradually becomes more like her dad's—lacking in warmth, sincerity, and directness. She begins to worry about impressing her classmates and teachers, or even Dad, just as Dad worries about impressing his boss. Her teachers probably don't help a lot. In junior high, a teacher assigns the class a theme about summer vacation and insists that the composition be at least 800 words. This encourages Jane to use two or three words where one would do the job, to stretch out her composition to the 800-word minimum set by the teacher. So what might have been an interesting, tightly written 500-word piece about a trip to Disney World turns out to be just another example of dull, flabby prose, mediocre at best. And Dad wonders why a bright kid like Jane doesn't get A's in English.

In addition to all this, Jane and Mr. Smith read so much bloated writing that they emulate, unconsciously, the style that seems to be the norm. Even if they were fortunate enough to have good writing instruction in school, they allow hard-learned skills to rust. They lose confidence in their ability to write clearly and convincingly. *They underestimate the power and grace of the simple, declarative sentence.* In desperation to get their points across, they resort to using more words on the theory that if one word is good, two are twice as good.

Far from contributing to the reader's enlightenment, wordiness enshrouds meaning in a fog of confusion. The late Professor Wilson Follett, one of America's foremost authorities on usage, called wordiness a vice. Here is what he wrote about it in *Modern American Usage*:

[T]o eliminate the vice of wordiness is to ensure the virtue of emphasis, which depends more on conciseness than on any other factor. Wherever we can make twenty-five words do the work of fifty, we halve the area in which looseness and disorganization can flourish, and by reducing the span of attention required we increase the force of thought. To make our words count for as much as possible is surely the simplest as well as the hardest secret of style.

If you want to write better, you will pay special heed to Professor Follett's advice. Cutting the fat is probably the quickest and surest way to improve. No matter how good your grasp of grammar, punctuation, spelling, and other fundamentals, you cannot write well unless you train yourself to write with fewer words. This chapter suggests some techniques for reducing verbal clutter and provides opportunities for practice in doing so. As you continue, remember this: Editing someone else's writing is easy. Editing your own takes discipline. Most of the time you'll have to be your own editor.

From Pleonasm to Verbosity

Now you might reasonably ask, "Does all this mean we must squeeze from our writing every single unnecessary word? The answer to that is a resounding "yes and no." What is "necessary"? In the opening sentence of this paragraph, we use the expression "every single." Is *single* really necessary? And is *really* necessary in the sentence that precedes this one? In each instance the word adds emphasis. Arguably, the sentences would be equally forceful without these emphatic words.

Words that when strictly construed do not add to meaning might be included for cadence or balance. An ear for the rhythm of prose, which becomes more sensitive with practice, guides the experienced writer in the placement of such words. Reading your own work aloud, or having someone read it to you, can help you train your ear. The use of extra words in this manner is called pleonasm. Although it is relatively harmless, it can be a sign of "creeping verbosity" and for that reason a writer should be aware of it. When you find yourself writing "really necessary," ask yourself whether *really* really *is* necessary. If it isn't, strike it out. This kind of critical self-appraisal can salvage bad writing and make good writing better.

Unlike pleonasm, verbosity is a serious fault. Consider what happens to the simple word *now* in the hands of a writer who does not appreciate the power of simplicity:

☆

N O W
AS OF NOW
AT PRESENT
AT THIS POINT
AT   THE   PRESENT
AT THE PRESENT TIME
AT THIS POINT IN TIME
AT THIS PARTICULAR POINT
AT THIS VERY POINT IN TIME
AT THIS PARTICULAR POINT IN TIME
IS
IS
IS
IS IS IS IS IS

What we have resembles a Christmas tree loaded with ornaments, but these "ornaments," far from being festive, are ugly and pretentious. They all signify a state of being in the present tense and therefore rest upon the word *is*. They all mean "now."

Everything on the tree between *now* and *is* adds nothing but clutter. Even *now*, when paired with *is*, may be pleonastic. It does, however, show how an extra word can emphasize a point. In the sentence "This morning, Matilda was sick, but now she is feeling better," *now* emphasizes the improvement in Matilda's condition between this morning and now. Omitting *now* from the dependent clause would weaken the sentence.

Verbosity is pleonasm taken to extremes. Asked to provide a new opening sentence for the Bible, a writer addicted to excess verbiage might offer something like this:

> At the very outset, our Maker successfully and effectively fabricated Heaven and all of the various planets of the whole universe, including, but not limited to, the planet Earth, on a timely basis.

William Shakespeare, in the speech of one of his characters, a simpleton, poked fun at verbosity: "The young gentleman according to fates and destinies, in such odd sayings the sisters three, and such branches of learning, is indeed deceased, or as you would say in plain terms, gone to heaven."

Saying "in plain terms" what you want to say is what low-fat writing is all about. As William Zinsser, the author, teacher, and journalist, wrote in *On Writing Well*, "Writing improves in direct ratio to the things we can keep out of it that shouldn't be there."

TEST YOURSELF

Cutting fat from your writing may not be as easy as it sounds. Take out your word cleaver and try your hand at simplifying the sentences below by eliminating unneeded words. Do no rewriting, except perhaps to supply one word to replace several:

1. The stadium has ample parking space available for fans' automobiles.

2. There is no easy shortcut to learning how to play the game of bridge.

3. In the appendix in the back of the book you will find a complete list of all references to the author's earlier previous works.

4. The ability to express yourself well by means of the written word is an essential skill to have if you want to be successful in business.

5. She joined the company at a higher salary level than she had expected to receive at the time when she made application for the position.

6. Let's have a discussion on this particular issue sometime at a later date.

7. His first fiction novel was not a successful book in terms of sales, but after his second made the best-seller list, the first began to sell better than it had done previously.

8. It is necessary for all of the fire extinguishers in the entire complex to be inspected on a monthly basis.

9. In the very beginning, a diet and exercise program might not produce the results you expected from the start, but don't become discouraged.

10. There were a number of very important issues that were brought up and thoroughly discussed in detail during the meeting.

ANSWERS

Your fat-cutting efforts should have produced something like this:

1. The stadium has ample parking space ~~available for fans' automobiles~~.

2. There is no ~~easy~~ shortcut to learning ~~how to play the game of~~ bridge.

3. In the appendix ~~in the back of the book you will find~~ a ~~complete~~ list of ~~all~~ references to the author's ~~earlier~~ previous works.

4. The ability to ~~express yourself~~ **write** well ~~by means of the written word~~ is ~~an~~ essential ~~skill~~ to ~~have if you want to be successful~~ in business.

5. She joined the company at a higher salary ~~level~~ than she had expected to receive ~~at the time~~ when she ~~made application~~ **applied** for the position.

6. Let's ~~have a~~ discussion ~~on~~ this ~~particular issue sometime at a~~ later ~~date~~.

7. His first ~~fiction~~ novel was not ~~a~~ successful ~~book in terms of sales~~, but after his second made the best-seller list, the first began to sell better ~~than it had done previously~~.

8. ~~It is necessary for~~ **A**ll ~~of the~~ fire extinguishers in the ~~entire~~ complex ~~to~~ **must** be inspected ~~on a~~ monthly ~~basis~~.

9. ~~In the very beginning~~, **At first** a diet and exercise program might not produce the results you expected ~~from the start~~, but don't become discouraged.

10. ~~There were~~ **A** number of ~~very~~ important issues ~~that~~ were ~~brought up and thoroughly~~ discussed in detail during the meeting.

We composed the sentences for the above exercise, but the following is from a published source—the 1990 Annual Report of the Exxon Corporation. Edit it as you did the sentences:

FINANCIAL OVERVIEW

Over time, Exxon's consistently strong earnings performance has enabled the company to achieve and maintain a position of extraordinary financial strength and flexibility. For example, over the past 10 years, Exxon's internal cash generation from operations amounted to more than $100 billion. This, together with a moderate increase in debt leverage, permitted the corporation to finance an aggressive capital investment program while continuing a rising flow of dividends per share and purchasing nearly $16 billion worth of Exxon stock. During this 10-year period, Exxon's capital and exploration investments have totaled more than $90 billion. Our underlying financial strength has permitted us to take advantage of the numerous opportunities that have been available in the energy, chemicals and other businesses in which Exxon participates and to meet our commitment to being a leader in those businesses.

Strong financial performance begins with knowing what our businesses are and, equally important, what they are not . . . what we are good at and what is better left to others. Exxon is focused on its basic businesses and is devoted to quality investments, operations, products, and services in those businesses.

Quality investments are those that are both sound as individual projects and consistent with and supportive of the corporation's long-range business strategies. Selectivity is the key. Given the inherent marketplace uncertainties in our businesses, capital investments are tested to ensure that they will be economically sound even under severely adverse conditions.

The corporation also is engaged in a continuous program of divesting assets that do not perform adequately and do not hold promise of sufficient returns to us in the future. Funds generated in the process can be reinvested more productively.

Optimizing Exxon's financial structure is a continuous

process. In order to preserve an ability to respond to large unexpected developments, Exxon retains resilience as well as strength in its financial structure. A measure of the company's success in this process is the triple A rating Exxon has retained through the years. We are one of a very small number of publicly traded companies that have this highest of financial ratings. As a consequence, we continue to have the capability to borrow large sums on short notice at lowest cost and on the best terms and conditions available in the marketplace.

Exxon retains considerable flexibility to alter its financial structure. We have the ability to promptly raise more debt when needed and to reduce debt rapidly when a temporary surplus of funds occurs. Similarly, when the corporation generates funds beyond its immediate investment needs, it has the option of returning them to shareholders—through a long-standing, flexible share buy-back program.

Because Exxon is a premier company, its shareholders expect to be well-rewarded for their investment. In the decade of the 1980s, shareholders realized an 18 percent per year total return on their Exxon stock, which compares favorably with the 13 percent return for the average of all other major oil companies and 14 percent for Standard's & Poor's 500 stock index average. Exxon's dividends and stock price appreciation together have produced an attractive, well-balanced return for equity investors.

Dividend income is particularly important to many Exxon shareholders, so the company preserves a healthy dividend component in its return to shareholders. Since 1980, Exxon's annual dividends have almost doubled, from $1.35 per current share to a present annualized rate of $2.68 per share. Over this period, approximately 55 percent of Exxon's earnings were distributed to shareholders as dividends.

The massive size of the energy, chemical and mining industries and the prospect for future global growth in these businesses will continue to offer Exxon an impressive array of investment opportunities. The company's strong financial base and flexibility will enable it to take full advantage of those opportunities and thereby continue to offer its shareholders attractive investment prospects.

The Exxon text is not grossly fat, certainly not like the previous examples. Nevertheless, editing to reduce the fat content even more results in shorter, more readable copy. Bear in mind that this is not rewriting; it is simply editing.

FINANCIAL OVERVIEW

~~Over time,~~ Exxon's consistently strong ~~earnings~~ performance has enabled the company to ~~achieve and~~ maintain ~~a position of~~ extraordinary financial strength and flexibility. ~~For example,~~ Over the past 10 years, ~~Exxon's internal~~ cash ~~generation~~ from operations amounted to more than $100 billion. This, together with a moderate increase in debt ~~leverage~~, permitted the corporation to finance an aggressive capital investment program while ~~continuing a~~ (increasing) ~~rising flow of~~ dividends ~~per share~~ and purchasing nearly $16 billion worth of Exxon stock. During this ~~10-year~~ period, Exxon's capital and exploration investments ~~have~~ totaled more than $90 billion. Our ~~underlying~~ financial strength has permitted us to take advantage of ~~the numerous~~ opportunities ~~that have been available~~ in ~~the~~ energy, chemicals, and other businesses in which Exxon participates and to meet our commitment to ~~being a leader~~ leadership in those businesses.

Strong financial performance begins with knowing ~~what~~

~~our businesses are and, equally important, what they are not . . .~~ what we are good at and what is better left to others. Exxon is focused on its basic businesses and is devoted to quality investments, operations, products, and services ~~in those businesses~~.

Quality investments are those that are both sound as individual projects and consistent with ~~and supportive of~~ the corporation's ~~long-range business~~ strategies. Selectivity is the key. Given the inherent marketplace uncertainties in our businesses, ~~capital~~ investments are tested to ensure that they will be ~~economically~~ sound even under ~~severely~~ adverse conditions.

The corporation also ~~is engaged in a continuous program of divesting~~ *(continually divests)* assets that do not perform adequately and do not ~~hold~~ promise ~~of~~ sufficient returns ~~to us in the future~~. Funds generated in the process can be reinvested more productively.

~~Optimizing Exxon's financial structure is a continuous process. In order~~ To preserve an ability to respond to large unexpected developments, Exxon retains resilience as well as strength in its financial structure. A measure of the company's success ~~in this process~~ is the triple A rating Exxon has retained through the years. We are one of ~~a very small number of~~ *(the few)* publicly traded companies that have this highest of financial ratings. As a consequence, we continue to have the capability to borrow large sums on short notice, at lowest cost, and on the best terms ~~and conditions~~ available ~~in the marketplace.~~

Exxon ~~retains~~ (has) considerable flexibility to alter its financial structure. We ~~have the ability to promptly raise more debt~~ (can borrow quickly) when ~~needed and to~~ (we need cash, or) reduce debt rapidly when (we have) ~~a~~ tempo-rary surplus ~~of funds occurs~~. ~~Similarly,~~ When the corpora-tion generates funds beyond its immediate ~~investment~~ needs, it has the option of returning them to sharehold-ers—through a long-standing ~~, flexible~~ share buy-back program.

~~Because~~ Exxon ~~is a premier company, its~~ shareholders expect to be well-rewarded for their investment. In the ~~decade of the~~ 1980s, shareholders realized an 18 percent per year total return on their Exxon stock, which compares favorably with the 13 percent return for the average of all other major oil companies and 14 percent for Standard's & Poor's 500 stock index average. Exxon's dividends and stock price appreciation together have produced an attractive, ~~well-balanced~~ return ~~for equity investors.~~

Dividend income is particularly important to many Ex-xon shareholders, so the company ~~preserves~~ (pays) a healthy divi-dend ~~component in its return to shareholders.~~ Since 1980, Exxon's annual dividends have almost doubled, from $1.35 per current share to a present annualized rate of $2.68 ~~per share~~. Over this period, approximately 55 percent of Exxon's earnings were distributed to shareholders ~~as dividends.~~

The ~~massive size of the energy,~~ chemical and mining industries and ~~the~~ <ins>their</ins> prospect for ~~future~~ global growth ~~in these businesses~~ will continue to offer Exxon ~~an~~ impressive ~~array of~~ investment opportunities. The company's strong financial base and flexibility will enable it to take ~~full~~ advantage of those opportunities and ~~thereby~~ continue to offer its shareholders <ins>an</ins> attractive investment ~~prospects.~~

Now let's move beyond editing to rewrite a short passage. Below is a long, rambling sentence that appeared in a full-page advertisement in the *Wall Street Journal* under the heading "An Open Letter to President and Mrs. Clinton on Containing Health Care Costs." Before you begin to rewrite, analyze the sentence and identify the globs of fat:

If we are to truly rein in health care costs' explosive growth, it is imperative that your upcoming health care program recognize and incent [sic] the use of technologies and medical instrumentation that cut costs, and that the program does not shortsightedly cap the purchase of instrumentation or technology that may cost more up front, but can result in significant reductions in the overall cost of treating patients.

Our revision breaks the single sentence into three and reduces the number of words from sixty-eight to forty-six. Notice particularly how the tedious phrases "it is imperative that," and "can result in significant reductions" shrink to single words—"must" and "reduce." Notice also how many adjectives and adverbs are absent from the revision:

If your program is to stop the growth of health care costs, it must provide incentives for the use of cost-cutting medical technologies. To cap the purchase of such technologies would be shortsighted. They may cost more initially, but they can reduce treatment costs significantly.

Use Adverbs and Adjectives Sparingly

The Elements of Style, by William Strunk, Jr., and E. B. White, may be the most popular book on writing and usage ever published—until this one, of course. Strunk and White advise: "Write with nouns and verbs, not adjectives and adverbs. The adjective has not been built that can pull a weak or inaccurate noun out of a tight spot."

If you develop the habit of choosing vivid nouns and strong verbs, you'll find yourself less often casting about for adjectives and adverbs to strengthen your sentences. If you become conscious of modifiers as you read and write, you may be astounded at how often they can be eliminated without loss of meaning or power. You almost surely will gain a new respect for nouns and verbs. In the following example, modifiers are printed in italic type:

> Include *all the* information *necessary* to support *your* point, but don't throw in *unnecessary* or *irrelevant* details. *Even one single obvious* exaggeration can make *your* readers *suspicious* of *your entire* presentation. *Clearly* distinguish between *personal* opinion and *actual* fact.

The passage contains thirty-nine words, of which seventeen are adjectives or adverbs. We can eliminate *thirteen* without doing violence to the message. That reduces by 33 percent the number of words in the passage. Think how much productivity in America might improve if all reading matter could be made 33 percent shorter without any loss of meaning. Here is the passage with the thirteen modifiers removed:

> Include information to support *your* point, but don't throw in *irrelevant* details. Exaggeration can make readers *suspicious* of *your* presentation. Distinguish between opinion and fact.

The passage is stronger with fewer modifiers, but if you feel that it wants emphasis, go ahead and put a couple of modifiers back in. For example, inserting *all* before *information* in the first sentence would stress the need for completeness. The purpose of this discussion is not to disparage adjectives and adverbs; it is to make you conscious of the fact that they are often unnecessary.

On a telecast of the Miss Teen U.S.A. pageant, the emcee gushed about the "fabulously wonderful" prizes awaiting the winner. Although verbal overkill is expected in such momentous events as beauty contests for teenagers, we venture to suggest that *wonderful* would have been sufficient. *Fabulous*, after all, derives from the Latin *fabula* (story or fable) and connotes something made up.

Now, words in modern English have not always kept their ancestors' meanings. Still, words like *fabulous*, *wonderful*, *fantastic*, *marvelous*, *terrific*, and *incredible* have lost much of their power because of overexposure. Use them sparingly. Give your readers the meat and let them pour on the gravy.

Adverbs seem to cause modifier pollution more than adjectives. During the early part of this century, boys and girls grew up devouring fourteen million copies of the adventures of Tom Swift. Tom was a sterling young hero who survived one harrowing adventure after another.

In the course of each story, Tom and his friends and enemies never just said something; they always said it excitedly or sadly or hurriedly. In the 1960s, the novels inspired their own genre of jokes, known as Tom Swifties. The object is to match the adverb with the quotation itself to produce a pun:

"I love pancakes," Tom said flippantly.

"Let's go to McDonald's," Tom said archly.

"I lost my flower," Tom said lackadaisically.

In addition to providing pun fun, Tom Swifties poke fun at the overuse of adverbs. We can have some fun today with sentences like this one, from a newspaper feature story: "An avid skydiver, he has jumped *successfully* twenty-seven times." Not as funny, but just as illustrative are: "He *willingly* agreed to be photographed"; "The pharmaceutical company that *successfully* develops a vaccine for AIDS will reap huge profits"; "She *actively* solicits funds for any worthwhile project"; and "The senator spoke *openly* in favor of the tax increase in a speech last week."

Can a person *un*willingly agree? Can a drug company *un*successfully develop a vaccine? Can a woman *in*actively solicit funds? Can a senator make a speech in favor of something without doing so openly? No. Yet such adverbial redundancies are commonplace.

Let Nouns Be Nouns ... Most of the Time

We learned in grammar school that a noun is a word that denotes a person, place, or thing. Some examples of nouns are *kitchen*, *bus*, *school*, *apple*, *television*, and *window*. No argument, right? But, in "kitchen cabinet," "bus driver," "school bus," "apple pie," "television station," and "window pane," the words are adjectives, for each modifies a noun and tells "what kind of."

In many cases, converting nouns to adjectives is not only acceptable but necessary if we are to avoid cumbersome phrases such as "a cabinet installed in a kitchen," "a bus for transporting children to school," "a pie made of apples," and so on. But, what about "emergency situation," "shower activity," and "slum areas"? *Voilà!* Serviceable nouns have changed to adjectives in the blink of an eye. The resulting expressions say nothing that *emergency*, *showers*, and *slums* don't say. They are therefore pleonastic.

Nouns converted to adjectives are especially offensive when they're forged into chains. In such constructions, the noun-adjectives modify each other. The financial report of a company laments "United States sales representative recruiting difficulty." Read the following pair of sentences aloud:

This year, the company has had United States sales representative recruiting difficulty.

This year, the company has had difficulty recruiting sales representatives in the United States.

Your ear should tell you immediately what is wrong with the first sentence. Its awkwardness comes across clearly. The second sounds better because it is more natural. It mimics the cadence of speech.

No doubt you've noticed that the second sentence is slightly longer than the first, and you might wonder why this example is included in a chapter on cutting fat. It's true that the first is shorter, but it *seems* longer. How can that be? The answer is simple. In the first sentence, the reader or listener must, in effect, redefine each of the nouns that have been converted to adjectives. Stated another way, you know subconsciously that *United States*, *sales*, and *representative* are nouns. When they are used as adjectives, your mind must make the adjustment before you can go on. Yes, some defend the construction of noun chains as a way to save words. But at what cost?

A company's personnel manager who issues an "employee advancement opportunity notification bulletin" instead of a "bulletin to notify employees of advancement opportunities" has, indeed, saved a few words, but at the expense of the manager's (and the company's) humanity.

POINTS TO PONDER AND REMEMBER

☞ The surest and fastest way to learn to write better is to learn to write fat-free.
☞ Never underestimate the power and grace of the simple, declarative sentence.

☛ If writing were "show and tell," verbs and nouns would be the "show," adverbs and adjectives the "tell." It is always better to show than to tell.

☛ Make every word earn the right to be there. If a word does not serve a useful function, cut it out.

☛ Just as a machine should have no unnecessary parts, a sentence should have no unnecessary words, a paragraph no unnecessary sentences.

▫ 5 ▫

Where the Action Is

Now that you have been taught the importance of the craft of fat-free writing, it's time for you to receive some instruction on how more energy can be put into your writing. Whoa! Let's try that again: *Now that you know how to write fat-free, you're ready to learn how to make your writing more energetic.*

Fat writing lacks energy. It huffs and puffs its way from phrase to phrase, sentence to sentence, paragraph to paragraph like an out-of-shape jogger trying to make it up a hill. The reader might wonder where it's heading and doubt that it will ever get there. But verbosity is not the only cause of sluggish writing. Our first sentence is flabby, but it also violates other principles of energetic writing. In this chapter we will examine those principles. We'll take you where the action is. We'll talk mainly about verbs—choosing them and using them—but we'll also discuss other ways to add energy to what you write.

We begin by sharing a paragraph from *The Man from St. Petersburg*, a novel of international intrigue by a master of the genre, Ken Follett:

> The motor car turned into the gravel forecourt and came to a noisy, shuddering halt opposite the door. Exhaust fumes drifted in through the window, and Walden held his breath. The driver got out, wearing helmet, goggles and a heavy motoring coat, and opened the door for the passenger. A short man in a black coat and felt hat stepped down from the car. Walden recognized the man and his heart sank: the peaceful summer afternoon was over.

Writers of that kind of fiction cannot afford sluggish prose. Readers don't buy their books as a cure for insomnia. Now look at a brief passage from *The Litigious Society*, by J. K. Lieberman:

> Justice Powell's concern is that courts not be burdened with every case in which a claim can plausibly be pressed that harm similar to the psychological trauma of suspension may be suffered.
>
> A tenable distinction can be drawn between the suspension case and Justice Powell's parade of horrors. In the case at hand, due process was invoked for discipline—punishment. Traditionally, due process has required a hearing whenever it is necessary to ascertain whether the conduct actually occurred for which the punishment is meted out.

We can learn by comparing the two passages. In Follett's, all the verbs are in the active voice, and only one—*was*, in the last sentence—derives from *to be*. Lieberman's contains several passive constructions and other verb faults, not to mention a bit of sinful syntax, which we will discuss in a later chapter. In fairness to Mr. Lieberman, however, we acknowledge that subject matter dictates style to some extent and that his book, taken as a whole, is not badly written.

The Horse versus the Cart

Voice is a grammatical term that you need to know. It refers to the relationship of a verb to its subject. If the subject is the doer, the verb is in the active voice. If the subject is the receiver, the verb is in the passive voice. The subject of an active-voice verb acts; the subject of a passive-voice verb is acted upon. The hoary admonition "Don't put the cart before the horse" makes a good memory-jogger. In "The horse pulls the cart," the verb is in the active voice because the horse (the subject) is acting (pulling). In "The cart is pulled by the horse," the verb is passive because the subject (cart) is acted upon (pulled).

Do the two sentences say the same thing? Technically, yes. But important differences intrude. A cart is wood and metal; it has no energy of its own. A horse is muscle and bone; it can walk, canter, gallop, and, yes, pull. Four words tell us what the horse is doing to the cart, but seven are required to tell us what the cart is having done to it.

So, for the moment at least, let's heed the advice our mother gave us and keep old Dobbin in front of the cart where he belongs. Your writing will be more energetic. Besides, whoever heard of a horse pushing a cart?

To illustrate how you make writing clearer, more concise, and more energetic by letting the horse do the work, we have revised the passage from the Lieberman book:

> Justice Powell fears that a deluge of cases in which litigants press the claim that they might suffer harm similar to the psychological trauma of suspension could burden courts.
>
> We can draw a tenable distinction between the suspension case and Justice Powell's parade of horrors. In the case at hand, the court invoked due process for discipline—punishment. Traditionally, due process requires a hearing when the court must ascertain whether the conduct for which punishment is meted out actually occurred.

By eliminating the passive constructions and engaging in a little judicious (pun intended) sentence recasting, we produced a slightly shorter and substantially more energetic passage.

In passive constructions, the agent of the action—that

is, the doer—is often omitted. That is why the passive voice is often called "the nobody voice." For example, in "The man was shot as he ran from the bank," the writer neglects to tell us who shot the man. A bank guard? A policeman? A little old lady who packed a .44 Magnum in her shopping bag? We must know the answer if we want to convert the sentence from passive to active. Writers addicted to passive constructions are more likely to forget to give readers pertinent information than are writers who rely mainly on the active voice.

For practice, read the following sentences and decide how you can convert them from passive to active constructions:

   a. Johnny was shot by Frankie.
   b. The reason capital gains are taxed at a lower rate is that capital gains are different from ordinary income.
   c. Simone's writing is rated better than the writing of her colleagues.
   d. Another problem with the book is the absence of data in support of the main positions taken by the author.
   e. The apartment complex was designed, financed, built, and leased, all within a year.

The first sentence is easy: "Frankie shot Johnny." To convert the second and third, you must supply doers. Who taxes capital gains? Who rates Simone's writing?

The fourth sentence contains four prepositional phrases. Prepositional phrases are often a by-product of the passive voice. A straightforward statement eliminates the prepositions and converts the sentence from sluggish passive to vigorous active: "The author fails to supply data to support his position." We do not need "Another problem," because we have used a stronger subject *(author)* and a stronger verb *(fails)*. We know from the context that a book, not an article or some other work, is what the discussion is about.

You can see a similar string of energy-draining prepositional phrases in the sentence that opened this chapter—the "rejected" one:

> Now that you have been taught the importance [OF] the craft [OF] fat-free writing, it's time [FOR] you to receive some instruction [ON] how more energy can be put [INTO] your writing.

The "accepted" opener has no prepositions. Prepositional phrases are not bad *per se*, but too many of them, especially strung together, may tell you that your sentence is wheezing along instead of running.

The Voice of Choice

No, we didn't forget the fifth sentence, (**e.**). You may still be scratching your head over that one. It has four different actions (verbs) all with the same receiver (the apartment complex), and the reader understands that each action has a different doer. Converting the sentence to the active voice would require something like "An architect designed the new apartment complex, the mortgage company financed it, the contractor built it, and the real estate broker leased it, all within a year." Not even the most passionate devotee of the active voice would accept such tedium.

This leads us to an important point. Having trashed the passive in the past few pages, let us now rise to its defense by mentioning some instances in which the passive is desirable or necessary. Clearly, we can use the passive voice if the actor is unknown or irrelevant. "The car was stolen six months ago" rightly focuses on the car, since the thief is unknown. Attributing the deed to "a thief" or "someone" is vague and serves no useful purpose. Similarly, "The pyramids were built thousands of years ago" cannot logically be expressed in the active voice, because we don't know who built the pyramids.

Sentence **e.** demonstrates that the passive voice sometimes helps us to avoid an awkward construction and that in some cases, the passive is even better than the active. Look again at the first sentence of our revision of the Lieberman passage: "Justice Powell fears that a deluge of cases in which litigants press the claim that they might suffer harm similar to the psychological trauma of suspension could burden courts." We wrote the sentence that way to demonstrate how a passive construction could be converted to active. Using the passive, however, makes the sentence easier to read:

> Justice Powell fears that courts might be burdened by a deluge of cases in which litigants press the claim that they could suffer harm similar to the psychological trauma of suspension.

The fault in the first revision lies in the long dependent clause, "that a deluge of cases in which litigants press the claim that they might suffer harm similar to the psychological trauma of suspension could burden courts." Twenty words stand between the subject *(deluge)* and the verb *(could burden)*, and readers must make their way through them to get the message. A lot of misunderstanding can take place in twenty words. Either version, though, is far more energetic than the original.

In our zeal to make our writing more energetic, we mustn't forget that our first duty as writers is to communicate. The ability to choose between the active and passive gives a writer flexibility to decide what to emphasize. In "The project was completed on time and under budget," the emphasis is on the project. The writer might not know or care who completed the project. Or perhaps the writer was responsible and was too modest to say, "I completed the project on time and under budget." On the other hand, if the project came in late and over budget, the writer might keep attention focused on the project by using the passive voice.

We can use the passive voice to mask or divide responsibility. "Taxes were raised five times in the past decade" and "Congress raised taxes five times in the past decade" are slightly different. Either way, your tax bill went up, but the passive version seems to take the heat off Congress. It leaves the reader with a different impression.

Good writers generally prefer the active voice to the passive voice because it is more vigorous, more interesting, and usually more concise. But good writers are not slavishly devoted to the active. They use the passive when it serves their purpose. The occasional, thoughtful use of the passive is not what sucks the life out of prose and puts the reader to sleep. The culprit is the awkward, purposeless, or too-frequent use of the passive.

Make the active voice the voice of choice when you write, but be flexible. Don't fear the passive. It is sometimes more natural and effective than the active.

Let Verbs Be Verbs . . . Most of the Time

Verbs are "where the action is." They are the spark plugs of sentences, and good writers prefer verbs to nouns. "Wait a minute!" you say. "That's like saying you prefer air to water. You can't live without either, and you can't write without using both nouns and verbs. So what's to prefer?"

You're right, of course; but let us explain. In the previous chapter we discussed the practice of turning nouns into adjectives and using them to modify other nouns. Now we're talking about converting verbs to nouns. In this process, the simple, direct, and strong verb *decide* becomes *make a decision*, trebling the number of words used to express the idea. Lawyers use a Latin term, *stare decisis*, to describe an established legal precedent. The phrase has an air of authority and finality that "The decision has already been made" lacks. When you write *decide*, you convey that feeling more strongly than when you write *make a decision*.

Writers who are uncomfortable with simple, direct ways

of saying things love verb-to-noun conversions. They also shy away from the active voice, overuse the verb *to be*, and leave big globs of fat floating around in their writing. Verb-to-noun conversions creep into the work of most writers, but writers who take pride in their work hunt them down and cut them out. With practice, you can become proficient at doing the same thing. It isn't easy, though. One writer we know uses the search key on his word processor to find words ending in *-ion*. Good idea, but not all verb-to-noun conversions end in *-ion*. Other common endings for them are *-ance*, *-ence*, *-ment*, and *-ed*. They often slither into phrases ending in prepositions. Their main distinguishing characteristic, however, is that they appear in phrases that begin with a verb and end with a noun that derives from a verb.

Look at a sample of your own work, or someone else's if you prefer, and mark all such verb phrases. Wherever possible, convert them into single verbs. Then reread the sample again and notice how much more vigorous it has become.

Before:	After:
bring to a conclusion	conclude
have a tendency	tend
make distribution	distribute
make provision	provide
take action	act
give a performance	perform
make reference	refer
commit an error	err
reach an agreement	agree
make application	apply
realized a profit	profited
draw to a close	close
use your imagination	imagine
come to the realization	realize
make an evaluation	evaluate
file a lawsuit	sue

Converting verbs to nouns is bad enough, but lately we have seen more and more examples of converting nouns to verbs. Cartoonist Bill Watterson noted this phenomenon in his brilliant *Calvin and Hobbes* comic strip. The conversation is between the precocious little boy, Calvin, and his friend Hobbes the tiger:

> **Calvin**: I like to verb words.
> **Hobbes**: What?
> **Calvin**: I take nouns and adjectives and use them as verbs. Remember when "access" was a thing? Now it's something you *do*. It got verbed. Verbing weirds language.

Calvin is right: "Verbing" does "weird" language. Of course, English has many useful words that are both nouns and verbs. You can right a wrong, wrong a friend, paddle your canoe with a paddle, paint with paint, love or make love, park your car and walk through the park, and so on. But the habit of indiscriminately converting one part of speech into another ought to be discouraged. A sportswriter for *The New York Times* writes that a second baseman who handled a pop fly casually "nonchalanted" the ball. Former secretary of state Alexander Haig loves terms like "contexting." The *Denver Post* quotes a city councilwoman as saying she would not be "guilted" into an idea. A columnist for the *Chicago Tribune* tells us that the democratic process has been "short-shrifted."

The English language comprises more than half a million words, and hundreds of useful new ones enter the language every year. But fabricated verbs such as the ones cited above serve no useful purpose. We ought to accept new words that add color or vigor, but let's short-shrift the ones that don't. We'd like to guilt some writers and speakers into the habit of using words better instead of creating mutants the language doesn't need.

There Are Verbs and Verbs

All five sentences that we used to illustrate converting passive constructions to active have something in common besides voice. Each relies on some form of the verb *to be*: *was*, *are*, *is*, *is*, and *was*, in that order. Often, though not always, the passive voice and the verb *to be* go together. *To be*, in all its forms, is the weakest of verbs in our language. It does not describe an action; it merely denotes existence.

We cannot write without *to be* verbs, but whenever we pass them by in favor of stronger verbs, we make our writing more vigorous. For example, "Hundreds of angry people were in the street" is weaker than "Hundreds of angry people filled the street."

The strongest verbs describe everyday actions. Verbs such as *run, cry, scream, spring, ooze, leak, roar, stink*, and *burst* evoke images of flesh-and-blood creatures. Verbs such as *represent, indicate, transpire, postulate, cogitate, surmise, ascertain*, and *fabricate*—although they have their uses—are lifeless and colorless.

Nouns that describe concepts also lack life and color. An active verb can often replace a concept noun. Take as an example the noun *disbelief*, as in "Disbelief was most people's reaction to the senator's statement." "Most people thought the senator was lying" might be too strong for your taste, but it's a more vigorous, "gutsy" way to say it. Concept nouns often require forms of *to be*, as did the first sentence. "Hank Aaron was given a standing ovation by 50,000 fans when he hit the home run that broke Babe Ruth's record" tells the story of that memorable event, but "Fifty thousand fans sprang to their feet and cheered" almost puts you in the stadium. *Standing ovation* is a concept. It doesn't do justice to the occasion. It *tells* when it ought to *show*.

Delete Your Expletives

No, we're not suggesting you bowdlerize your writing. We're talking about a different kind of expletive. In grammar, an expletive is a word that temporarily takes the place of a subject or an object. For example, in "It is believed that this book will help you write better," *it* is an expletive. In "There are few people who cannot improve," *there* is an expletive. *It* and *there* appear to be subjects of *is* and *are*, but they cannot be called true subjects. Some grammarians call expletives "dummy subjects." The true subject of an expletive construction may or may not appear later in the sentence.

America became conscious of the word *expletive* during the Watergate hearings. In published transcripts of Oval Office conversations among President Richard Nixon and his aides, ellipsis points and the parenthetical "expletive deleted" were substituted for profanities. As a result, millions of people learned a new word. They did not, however, learn whether Mr. Nixon cussed imaginatively or whether his expletives were as ordinary as Mrs. Nixon's Republican cloth coat.

In any event, far from being offensive, expletives of the kind we are discussing are allowed in polite society and appear regularly in family newspapers. But they are not always welcome in lively prose. Several expletive constructions in succession can rob your writing of energy and make it monotonous. When you can eliminate an expletive without saying anything that's awkward or outright barbarous, you ought to do so. In the two examples with which we introduced this discussion, eliminating the expletives would also get rid of the passive voice: "This book will help you write better," and "Most people can improve" are more succinct and vigorous.

We cannot eliminate all expletives, just as we cannot eliminate all passive constructions and all uses of the verb *to be*. Even if we could, we wouldn't want to, for they are often desirable and sometimes necessary. You should be aware, however, that they can sap vitality from your work. Writers who cannot digest direct, forceful statements often thrive on expletives.

TEST YOURSELF

Rewrite the sentences that you believe need to be more energetic. Remember to watch for verb-to-noun conversions, passive constructions, and expletives:

1. It said in the annual report that three new directors were elected by shareholders this year.

2. It is raining.

3. Application has already been made for a construction permit.

4. The dog had been beaten mercilessly, and it was given treatment by a veterinarian who was there by chance.

5. There was much fear of espionage during World War II even though there was little chance that the United States would be invaded by the Germans.

6. It is sunny but cold today.

7. "There you go again," Carter said to Reagan.

8. It is better to have loved a short man that never to have loved a tall.

9. There was little demand for the product, so the store manager ordered its removal from the inventory.

10. There is no money in this year's budget for construction of a new school.

11. There are the two men we saw coming out of the bank.

12. After they have made a study of the alternatives, our engineers will make recommendations for revisions.

--- ANSWERS ---

Here are our revisions and comments. Keep in mind that most of the sentences can be revised in more than one way. Don't be concerned if your revisions are not like ours. The important thing is for you to recognize the passives, expletives, and verb-to-noun conversions and understand how they affect the sentences. Revisions are in italics; comments, if any, are in parentheses.

1. *According to the annual report, shareholders elected three new directors this year.*

2. (We know of no better way to say this. Technically, *it* is an indefinite pronoun, not an expletive in this example.)

3. *The contractor has already applied for a construction permit.* (We must supply a subject to eliminate the passive.)

4. *Some s.o.b. had beaten the dog mercilessly, and a veterinarian who was there by chance treated it.* (Again, we supplied a subject because the person who had beaten the dog was unspecified. The only certainty was that the dog-beater was, indeed, an s.o.b.)

5. *Americans feared espionage during World War II, but the United States stood little chance of being invaded by the Germans.* (The active construction is shorter and stronger.)

6. *The day is sunny but cold.*

7. (Actually, Reagan said that to Carter, but in either case, *there* is an adverb, not an expletive.)

8. (We like this one as it is.)

9. *The store manager removed the product from inventory because it was not much in demand.*

10. *This year's budget has no money for a new school.*

11. (This sentence does not need to be revised. *There* is not an expletive.)

12. *After they have studied the alternatives, our engineers will recommend revisions.*

Variety Is the Spice

The only sin greater than confusing your readers is boring them. If you want to put them to sleep, a succession of sentences of about the same length and style beats warm milk two to one.

Compare this:

Arriving at the edge of town, we came upon the shopping center we had been told about. Slowing down the car, we watched carefully for the store. Because it was set back from the road, we did not see it right away. Using his young eyes to good advantage, little Johnny was the first one of us to spot it. Anticipating an adventure in toyland, he was unable to contain his excitement. Bouncing up and down on the car seat, he screeched, "There it is! There it is!"

with this:

We reached the edge of town and found the shopping center. It was right where they said it would be—set well back from the road. Slowing down, we watched carefully for the store, but we didn't see it right away. Little Johnny spotted it. He was so excited he couldn't sit still. He began screeching, "There it is! There it is!," all the while bouncing on the car seat. He was looking forward to his adventure in toyland.

Give your readers a short sentence now and then. Startle them. Keep them awake. Then let them relax with a sentence that moves along smoothly but rhythmically, like the clackety-clack of train wheels.

Suspense writers know well how to do this. In *The Big Sleep*, Raymond Chandler wrote:

I didn't go near the Sternwood family. I went back to the office and sat in my swivel chair and tried to catch up on my foot-dangling. There was a gusty wind blowing in at the windows and the soot from the oil burners of the hotel next door was down-drafted into the room and rolling across the top of the desk like a tumbleweed drifting across a vacant lot. I was thinking about going out to lunch and that life was pretty flat and that it would probably be just as flat if I took a drink and that taking a drink all alone at that time of day wouldn't be any fun anyway. I was thinking this when Norris called.

Professional writers don't measure their sentences and consciously decide when it's time to put in a short one, a long one, or a differently constructed one. They just know. Their ear for rhythm, for the beautiful cadence of good prose, guides them. That's why they're good.

Many writing teachers advise their students to write in short sentences. We concur, but with some reservations. A succession of short sentences can be jarring to the reader. Choppy writing might not be boring, but it can make the reader feel under attack. Our advice is to keep your sentences on the short side most of the time, but don't hesitate to write a long one now and then if you can keep it under control. A long, flowing sentence can be soothing. A long, rambling sentence can be disconcerting.

Kick the Slackers off the Team

For a team, a committee, or a task force to do its best, all members must do their part. A group with just one slacker won't perform as well as it should, because part of its energy will be expended to support the slacker. The mission, whether it's to win a game, raise money for a charity, or develop a vaccine, may be jeopardized.

Writing is like that. A sentence is a team composed of words, a paragraph is a team composed of sentences, and so on. Slackers are lazy words that don't contribute much of anything to the message. They rob the team of the energy it needs. They are to writing what *you know* is to speaking. Examples are seemingly innocuous words and phrases such as *very, quite, in other words, rather, pretty much, sort of,* and *in a very real sense.* Most of the time, they don't do any real work, and they ought to be kicked off the team. Some of them, some of the time, do serve useful purposes—but not many and not often.

We call them "weasel words." When a weasel word

slithers its way into your writing, examine its function. If you can do without it, pop goes the weasel!

Clichés are also energy thieves. Clichés are tired words and phrases that might once have served honorably but should have been retired a century ago. They're especially common in business letters—*thanking you, I remain; enclosed please find; at your earliest convenience; per your request; pursuant to; thanking you in advance.* Let's give these and other grizzled veterans a long rest. They've earned it.

Next time you write a business letter, read it carefully before you lick the flap. If you find you have used a phrase you've seen in someone else's letter, cut it out and expend a little energy to come up with a good replacement.

POINTS TO PONDER AND REMEMBER

- ☛ Whoever heard of a horse pushing a cart?
- ☛ Make the active your voice of choice, but don't be a slave to it.
- ☛ Verbs are the spark plugs of good writing.
- ☛ Vary your sentences.
- ☛ Calvin says, "Verbing weirds language." So does "nouning."
- ☛ Lazy words are like lazy people. They don't do their part.

□ 6 □

Sinful Syntax

When lawmakers decide they need to extract more money from the populace, they usually look first at taxing beer, whiskey, and in at least one state, certain forms of horizontal recreation. The news media invariably call taxes on these commodities "sin taxes." Syntax, however, is not a tax on anything, save perhaps the patience of readers of prose that does not follow the principles of good syntax. And, at the risk of eternal *pun*ishment, we observe that pages of (bad) syntax is death.

Syntax can be complicated. Linguists have spent lifetimes in syntactical pursuits. For our purposes, however, a simple definition suffices: *Syntax is the arrangement of words and phrases into sentences to create meaning*. When sentence elements are not arranged according to the rules of syntax, meaning may be absent or obscure. For example, "Diana pie Charles threw at the" is a meaningless jumble of words. Arrange them in the right order and you get an understandable sentence—"Diana threw the pie at Charles" or "Charles threw the pie at Diana," depending on whether you choose Diana or Charles as the subject of your sentence. Obviously, a small difference in the arrangement creates a great difference in meaning. Although this example is flagrant, many writers fail to grasp the fundamentals of syntax.

The Seven Deadly Syntaxes

To illustrate the principles of good syntax, and have a bit of fun in the bargain, we have identified seven examples of bad syntax. We call them "The Seven Deadly Syntaxes"—*wandering modifiers, danglers, non sequiturs, faulty parallelism, unclear antecedents, sardine sentences*, and *rambling wrecks*.

THE FIRST DEADLY SYNTAX: WANDERING MODIFIERS

Adjectives and adverbs, including phrases and clauses used as modifiers, should be as close as possible to whatever they modify. When modifiers are turned loose and allowed to wander around in the sentence, confusion reigns.

The *Wall Street Journal* quoted a source as saying:

"Television's insatiable appetite for fresh grief eats up sobbing fire, flood or crime victims at horrendous rates."

Fire sometimes roars, rages, and crackles, but never, to our knowledge, does fire sob, yet that's what the sentence says—"sobbing fire." Placing the adjective *sobbing* where it belongs would have prevented a ludicrous statement:

"Television's insatiable appetite for fresh grief eats up sobbing victims of fire, flood or crime at horrendous rates."

The example also illustrates the perils of converting nouns to adjectives, as we discussed in Chapter 4. In the sentence above, *fire, flood*, and *crime* are nouns strung together into a chain and used as adjectives modifying *victims*. Letting these words play their proper role as objects of the preposition *of* prevents the bad syntax; or, to look at it another way, correcting the syntax forces the writer to let the nouns be nouns.

This example comes from the *Atlanta Constitution*:

> Southland Corp., the parent company of 7-Eleven Stores
> . . . announced it would no longer sell any men's magazines in April.

Does this mean that anyone wanting a copy of *Playboy* has to wait until May to buy it? The prepositional phrase *in April* is used as an adverb telling when the company made its announcement. *In April* belongs immediately after the verb *announced*.

An Associated Press article opened with this sentence:

> Bail was reduced Monday for a woman accused of fatally shooting the man accused of molesting her son in the courtroom.

Where was the son molested? Surely, not in the courtroom. That is where the woman shot the accused molester. The prepositional phrase *in the courtroom* is the wandering modifier. Moving it to the proper position yields:

> Bail was reduced Monday for a woman accused of shooting, in the courtroom, the man accused of molesting her son.

In each of the examples above, the reader can easily tell from the context what the writer intended, but misplaced modifiers often leave readers wondering:

> The senator said the committee chairman would decide whether to bring the matter up for a vote next Tuesday.

This sentence violates the first of the Five C's: It is unclear. Did the senator say that the committee chairman would *decide* next Tuesday, or that the matter might be brought to a vote next Tuesday? We don't know; we can only guess.

The little word *only* has had the wanderlust for so long

that few people seem to know where its home is supposed to be. Like other modifiers, *only* is best placed next to whatever it modifies, as in "The doctor can see you for only thirty minutes." *Only* is a word used to restrict something. In this sentence, it refers to the amount of time the doctor has available—*only* thirty minutes. Too often, a sentence like that will come out as "The doctor can only see you for thirty minutes." Does the writer or speaker intend to say that the only thing the doctor can do is *see* you? She can't hear you, shake your hand, treat you, tell your fortune, or join you for a quick drink.

The misplacement of *only* may not be a major cause of misunderstanding, but putting it where it belongs will make your writing more polished.

In Chapter 14, we discuss more fully the proper placement of *only.* Meanwhile, remember Smokey the Bear: "Only *you* can prevent forest fires." Move *only* to another location and you change the meaning. "You can only prevent forest fires" means you cannot do anything *but* prevent them. You can't start them or extinguish them. "You can prevent only forest fires" means you can prevent nothing but forest fires.

Smokey has the syntax right: Only you can prevent misplaced modifiers.

Adjectives usually precede the words they modify, as in "the good book," "the blue sky," "the seven hills of Rome." Adverbs may precede or follow, depending on the usage. An ear for natural word order is the writer's best guide. Compare these sentences:

> The bride slowly walked down the aisle.

> The bride walked slowly down the aisle.

The first sentence is not wrong, but the second is better. The word order in the second is the more natural and more emphatic. The word order in the first sentence seems to lead the reader to emphasize *walked*; in the second, the emphasis is on *slowly,* where it belongs. In a sentence such as "Marjorie often eats two or three watermelons a week," the adverb *often* falls naturally before its verb, *eats.* "Marjorie eats often two or three watermelons a week" is almost nonsensical. Beginning with *often* would create an unmistakable shift of emphasis.

Skillful writers choose the natural word order whenever they can, but they know when they should depart from it. Natural word order can sometimes be reversed for dramatic effect. "I entered the Oval Office, and there was the president of the United States standing by the window" is less dramatic than "I entered the Oval Office and there, standing by the window, was the president of the United States." In the first example, the sentence tails off, ending not with a bang but a window. The second leaves the reader with a clear picture. The end of a sentence is the point of greatest emphasis.

The guiding principle in the placement of modifiers is this: *No reader should have to read a sentence twice to get its meaning or its full effect.*

THE SECOND DEADLY SYNTAX: DANGLERS

A dangler is a phrase that seems to be looking for, but not finding, something to modify. With some danglers, there is simply nothing they *can* modify. With others, the word or words they should modify are too far away for the reader to make a connection. The most common dangler is the infamous but misnamed dangling participle. A dangling participle actually involves a participial phrase—a phrase beginning with a participle and placed near or attached to something it cannot logically modify.

A participle is a verb form used as an adjective. Most participles end in *-ing*, but some end in *-ed* or *-en*—*running* horse, *working* knowledge, *helping* hand, *wounded* animal, *molded* plastic, *broken* glass. Although a dangling participle can work mischief on meaning, most examples of this syntactical misfire are merely humorous. Here is the classic example:

> Walking along Marietta Street in downtown Atlanta, a statue of the famous editor Henry Grady caught my attention.

No doubt a walking statue of the venerable editor would catch your attention. In that sentence, the participial phrase has nothing to modify, since *statue* is the subject. To correct it, we must supply a new subject:

> Walking along Marietta Street in downtown Atlanta, I saw a statue of the famous editor Henry Grady.

This undangles the participle by putting it next to the word it logically relates to—in this case, *I*.

The next example seems to have the china shop taking revenge on the bull:

> Broken into a thousand pieces, the bull just snorted and paid no attention to the once-priceless china that littered the floor.

The dangler, *broken into a thousand pieces*, obviously should modify *china*, but the word is too far removed. One of several possible revisions:

> Broken into a thousand pieces, the once-priceless china littered the floor. The bull just snorted and paid no attention to it.

Next we have astronomers having been perfected after years of painstaking work (testimony, no doubt, to the value of on-the-job training):

> Perfected after years of painstaking work, astronomers say the new telescope will greatly aid in the study of our solar system.

The sentence should read something like this:

Astronomers say the new telescope, perfected after years of work, will greatly aid in the study of our solar system.

Dangling participles are most often introductory phrases, but they can come anywhere in a sentence. In this example, the offending participle comes at the end:

Speed limits must be strictly observed when driving in a school zone.

The participial phrase *driving in a school zone* has nothing to modify. To make the sentence correct, we eliminate the passive construction, *speed limits must be strictly observed*, and supply a subject for the participial phrase to modify:

When driving in a school zone, you must strictly observe speed limits.

A syntactical fault closely related to the dangling participle is the misplaced appositive. An appositive is a phrase that defines or clarifies whatever it is attached to. For example, in "We believe that Molly Malone, a civil engineer, should direct the project," the appositive is *a civil engineer*. It defines *Molly Malone* and could as easily be the subject of the sentence. Sometimes a syntactical sinner will render such a sentence as "A civil engineer, we believe the project should be directed by Molly Malone."

Words or phrases that express contrast are called negative appositives. For example, in "The states, not the federal government, bear the responsibility for controlling crime," the negative appositive is *the federal government*. A careless writer might say, "The states bear the responsibility for controlling crime, not the federal government."

An appositive, by definition, is always next to the word or phrase it describes. Moving an appositive to a different location will always produce sinful syntax.

Thoughtlessness, rather than ignorance, is most often the cause of danglers. In our haste we may neglect to read what we have written and thus overlook an error that makes us look—and feel—foolish.

Additional practice in recognizing and repairing sentences with danglers is included in Chapter 14.

THE THIRD DEADLY SYNTAX: NON SEQUITURS

Non sequitur is a Latin term meaning "it does not follow." In the study of logic, a non sequitur is a conclusion that does not flow from the premise. In syntax, a non sequitur is a statement that is irrelevant or illogical when we consider what follows it. For example, in "Born in Spain, Ballesteros won the golf tournament by seven strokes," *born in Spain* stands in apposition with *Ballesteros*. But what is the connection? There is none. If we write, "Born in Spain, Ballesteros as a boy aspired to be a bullfighter," the reader can logically infer a connection between the golfer's birthplace and his boyhood aspiration.

Non sequiturs occur most often at the beginning of a sentence, but they can occur elsewhere. In this sentence, the non sequitur is the long appositive describing Mrs. O'Leary:

> For the second consecutive year, the blue ribbon for the best cake was won by Mrs. O'Leary, a tall, angular woman who holds a degree in anthropology and is a veteran of the civil rights movement of the 1960s.

Non sequiturs violate no "rule" of grammar or syntax. They rarely confuse the reader. They just don't belong in stylish writing. If pieces of information are together syntactically, they ought to be related in meaning or function. As your appreciation for simple, clear expression grows, you will be less inclined to use non sequiturs.

THE FOURTH DEADLY SYNTAX:
FAULTY PARALLELISM

The principle of parallelism, or parallel construction, is this: *If sentence elements are parallel in meaning, they should be parallel in grammatical construction.* A sentence such as "He likes hunting, fishing, and to swim" is an obvious example of faulty parallelism. The series comprises two gerunds and one infinitive, all used as objects of *likes*. There is nothing subtle about it. It offends the ear like a bass fiddle in the violin section.

Parallelism in its more subtle forms is not an easy concept to get across, but paying attention to it can help you to write with style and grace. The Preamble to the Constitution is a single, beautifully crafted sentence beginning:

> We the people of the United States, in order to *form* a more perfect union, *establish* justice, *provide* for the common defense, *promote* the general welfare, and *secure* the blessings of liberty . . .

Notice how the parallel elements (italicized) are expressed as parallel grammatical units—verb phrases. Suppose it had been written with no attention to parallelism:

> We the people of the United States, in the interest of forming a more perfect union, to establish justice, make certain our common defense as well as the general welfare is provided for, and that liberty's blessings are made secure . . .

The meaning has not changed, but the effect is jarring. Grace, style, and rhythm have disappeared along with the parallelism.

Parallelism might also be called balance. Unbalanced writing, which is to say writing with faulty parallelism, makes readers vaguely uncomfortable. The correlative pair *either* . . . *or* illustrates the point. Think of an old-fashioned scale such as druggists once used. For the scale to balance, the contents of one side must weigh the same as the contents of the other. When you writer *either . . . or*, the "weight," or grammatical form, of the information paired with *either* must be the same as that of the information paired with *or*. In "Pierre has either gone fishing or someone has taken him to the movies," the elements of *either* are not parallel with the elements of *or*. To eliminate the faulty parallelism, simply start the sentence with *either*: "Either Pierre has gone fishing or someone has taken him to the movies."

When you construct a series, the items in it must be of the same part of speech if you want to maintain good balance. In "Carmen is talented, intelligent, and attractive," the series is properly balanced. "Carmen is talented, intelligent, attractive, and plays a good game of golf" is a "phony" series because *plays a good game of golf* is not parallel with *talented*, *intelligent*, and *attractive*, which are adjectives. "Carmen is talented, intelligent, and attractive, and she plays a good game of golf" is correct because *she plays a good game of golf* is not part of the series. It is an independent clause joined to the main clause by the conjunction *and*.

Here is a good example of a series in which faulty parallelism causes ambiguity:

> The chairman told the shareholders that sales volume dropped sharply in the fourth quarter, that revenues would be less than in the previous year, and the price of the company's stock declined by twenty percent as a result.

The reader does not know whether the chairman told the shareholders that the company's stock declined as a result of the bad news, or whether the writer was observing that the stock price dropped because of the chairman's remarks. If the former was the case, *that* should be inserted before *the* in the last clause, making the series elements parallel. If the latter possibility was what happened, *the price of the company's stock declined by twenty percent as a result* should not be part of the series. In that case, the sentence should be recast somewhat like this:

The chairman told the shareholders that sales volume dropped sharply during the fourth quarter and that revenues would be less than in the previous year. As a result of the chairman's remarks, the price of the company's stock declined by twenty percent.

Writers who neglect parallelism put at risk both grace and clarity.

THE FIFTH DEADLY SYNTAX: UNCLEAR ANTECEDENTS

A pronoun is a word that takes the place of a noun, but a pronoun cannot stand alone. It must have an antecedent— a noun that comes before it and defines it—otherwise, the reader will not know what noun the pronoun replaced. In a sentence such as "I saw the movie and liked it," we know that *it* stands for *movie.* An antecedent need not be in the same sentence; it can appear in a preceding sentence. In this pair of sentences, "I saw *Gone with the Wind* three times. I think it is the best movie ever made," *Gone with the Wind* is the antecedent of *it.* An antecedent need not be in the *immediately* preceding sentence, but the farther it is from the pronoun, the greater the possibility of ambiguity.

To prevent ambiguity, you must make the identity of the antecedent unmistakable. "Marjorie asked Elizabeth whether she was invited to the party," leaves us wondering what Marjorie wants to know. We cannot be certain about the antecedent of *she.* If the antecedent is *Marjorie,* then Marjorie is asking about her own invitation. If the antecedent is *Elizabeth,* Marjorie is asking about Elizabeth's invitation. In "Kevin asked Carlos if he could play shortstop," it is not clear whether Kevin is asking for permission to play shortstop or whether he's inquiring about Carlos's ability to play the position.

Although an antecedent is, by definition, a word or

words that *precede* a pronoun, writers sometimes vary their sentence structure by putting the antecedent *after* the pronoun. It is common and, in many cases, acceptable, to place the antecedent *after* the pronoun. The preceding sentence provides the example. The pronoun is *it*; the antecedent (an infinitive) that tells us what *it* refers to is *to place*. Keep in mind, though, that this kind of construction increases the chance of ambiguity. Use it carefully, if at all.

Attorneys and others who must write with legal precision must be especially wary of unclear antecedents. If a legal document is unclear, it is open to interpretation, and the interpretation the document receives may not be the one the writer intended. This is why legal documents contain words like *said* and *aforementioned*—for example, *said contract*, *aforementioned settlement*, and so on. These expressions eliminate the need for the possibly ambiguous pronoun *it*.

In nonlegal writing, you might need to recast the sentence or repeat the noun to prevent ambiguity caused by an unclear antecedent. For example, in "Take the candy from the box if you're going to give it to Miguel," we cannot be certain whether *it* refers to *candy* or *box*. The sentence might be rendered either "If you're going to give the candy to Miguel, take it from the box" or "Take the candy from the box if you're going to give the candy to Miguel." The first version is preferable.

Additional practice in recognizing and repairing sentences with unclear or ambiguous pronoun references is included in Chapter 11.

THE SIXTH DEADLY SYNTAX:
SARDINE SENTENCES

Attempting to pack too many facts into one sentence, like sardines in a can, causes much bad writing. Here is a sardine sentence from *Newsweek*:

"Silent Cal has gotten a raw deal," says Rep. Silvio Conti, a Massachusetts Republican who persuaded the House to declare last week the first annual Calvin Coolidge Week, marking the 60th anniversary of his swearing-in after Warren G. Harding's death by his notary public father in the family home in Plymouth Notch, Vt.

Pity the readers on whom *Newsweek* inflicted that sentence. Let's analyze it. It says that last week marked the sixtieth anniversary of *his* swearing-in. Whose? Mr. Conti's? Not likely. President Coolidge's? Probably; but we can only infer that. The sentence also refers to Warren G. Harding's death "by his notary public father." Did the elder Mr. Harding bump off his son? The sentence is packed so full of information that the reader has trouble figuring out how each fact relates to the others.

The sentence contains fifty words. Some writers can handle long sentences; others can't. The *Newsweek* writer let the sentence get out of control. Our solution would be to break the multi-idea sentence into four one-idea sentences:

"Silent Cal has gotten a raw deal," says Rep. Silvio Conti. The Massachusetts Republican persuaded the House to declare last week the first annual Calvin Coolidge Week to mark the 60th anniversary of Coolidge's swearing-in. Coolidge succeeded to the presidency upon the death of Warren G. Harding. He was sworn-in by his father, a notary public, at the family home in Plymouth Notch, Vt.

Here is another example, the opening sentence of a news release distributed by a public relations firm to announce a change of address:

Paul Ridings Public Relations, Inc.—which became the first public relations firm in the Southwest to own it own building in 1956 when it bought the building at 3467 West Freeway where it had been a tenant for the year previous, starting July 1, 1955, when the first was founded—has moved.

We won't rewrite or critique this one; it isn't worth the bother. When you're tempted to add another fact to a sentence, remember that little dot on the bottom row of your keyboard. It's called a period. Use it.

THE SEVENTH DEADLY SYNTAX: RAMBLING WRECKS

How often have you listened to a speaker go on and on until you wanted to scream, "For Pete's sake, get to the point!"? Going on *ad infinitum, ad nauseam* to make a point is not limited to speakers. Writers do it too. Here is a rambling wreck of a sentence from a document titled "Public Research and Organizational Change":

> The trend in society toward a dissolution of divisions between the public and private sectors, toward a multi-institutional, knowledge-based global economy, and the increasing role that corporations are playing in employee training, development and education, and the pervasive need to communicate the constant, rapid social and economic changes that characterize the Information Age, are among the current pressures shaping the future of communications management.

We challenge you to sort out this sentence without reading it several times. By the time you reach the main verb (*are*, following *Information Age*), you are overwhelmed by the seemingly endless subject. The sentence is not only rambling, it is syntactically flawed in other ways.

A roundabout way of speaking or writing is called circumlocution. Abraham Lincoln might have begun his Gettysburg address by saying, "A long time ago, I think it must have been in the neighborhood of eighty-six or eighty-seven years ago—anyway, it was before my time—some of our forefathers, which is to say our ancestors, got together for a little meeting and . . ." But no rambling wrecker was Abe. Honest. He began with "Four score and seven years ago . . ." and thus ensured his place in the history of oratory as well as human rights.

TEST YOURSELF

Identify the syntactical sins in the following sentences and try to eliminate the problems, if any, by revising the sentences:

1. If your kitten will not drink cold milk, put it in the microwave oven for a few seconds.

2. Former hostage Terry Waite talked about his five years of confinement in Beirut with Barbara Walters.

3. After the congressman finished his speech, members of the audience asked questions, and they often showed strong bias in favor of the legislation.

4. The company hired a new law firm, an advertising agency, an accounting firm, and fired half of its management team.

5. The resources of the company were vast, but the owners were unable to use them to best advantage after they became tied up in litigation.

6. Carried to extreme, you can damage your health by strenuous exercise.

7. Unlike playing chess, bridge can be enjoyed in a party atmosphere.

8. An avid traveler, Sims never has a problem deciding how to spend his vacation.

9. An avid traveler, Sims has lived alone since his wife died ten years ago.

10. The young man was fired for sloppy work and drinking.

11. Due to the fluctuating price of silver, we can only guarantee the price of coins for ten days.

12. The 16–1 vote followed a grenade explosion in a crowd of Peace Now demonstrators outside a cabinet meeting that killed a paratrooper who friends said fought in the Lebanon invasion and injured nine others who demanded Sharon be fired.

—————————— Answers ——————————

Here are our comments and suggested revisions. Revisions are in italics; comments are in parentheses:

1. *If your kitten will not drink cold milk, warm the milk in the microwave oven for a few seconds.* (We have a choice of antecedents—the kitten or the milk. Pity the poor kitten if we failed to make the right choice.)

2. *Former hostage Terry Waite talked with Barbara Walters about his five years of confinement in Beirut.* (Perhaps Mr. Waite would have enjoyed being confined with the lovely and talented Ms. Walters, but not for five years—and certainly not in Beirut.)

3. *After the congressman finished his speech, members of the audience asked questions, and the questions often showed strong bias in favor of the legislation.* (This revision assumes that the writer intended to say that the questions, not the questioners, showed bias. It could go either way, depending on what the writer wanted to emphasize. A better version is *After the congressman finished his speech, members of the audience asked questions that often showed strong bias in favor of the legislation.*)

4. *The company hired a new law firm, an advertising agency, and an accounting firm, and fired half of its management team.* (This revision corrects faulty parallelism. The second *and* separates the series from *fired half of its management team*, which is not part of the series.)

5. *The resources of the company were vast, but the owners were unable to use them to best advantage after the resources were tied up in litigation.* (Again, we must make an assumption. We are assuming that the resources, not the owners, were tied up.)

6. *Carried to extreme, strenuous exercise can damage your health.* (Getting rid of the dangler makes a stronger and shorter sentence.)

7. *Unlike chess, bridge can be enjoyed in a party atmosphere.* (The revision makes the elements parallel.)

8. (No revision needed. We are justified in inferring a link between the appositive and Sims's vacation choices.)

9. (We are unable in this case to determine how the

opening appositive might be linked to the fact that Sims lives alone. If no such connection can be established, the two items of information should not be linked syntactically.)

10. *The young man was fired for sloppy work and for drinking.* (Was the young man fired for sloppy drinking? Inserting *for* before *drinking* prevents the reader's mind from trying to pair *drinking* with *sloppy.* The second *for* is unnecessary if we reverse the order of the reasons for the young man having been fired: "The young man was fired for drinking and sloppy work." Anomalies like that must be frustrating to foreigners trying to learn English.)

11. *Due to the fluctuating price of silver, we can guarantee the price for only ten days.* (By repositioning *only,* we make it clear that the modifier relates to *ten days.* Try moving *only* to other positions [indicated by *] and see how the meaning or emphasis changes with each move: *Due * to the fluctuating price of silver * , we can guarantee * the price of * the coins for ten days * .*)

12. *The 16–1 vote by the cabinet followed a grenade explosion in a group of Peace Now demonstrators demanding that Sharon be fired. The explosion killed a paratrooper who friends say fought in the Lebanon invasion. Nine other people were injured.* (The sardine sentence, from a UPI press dispatch, is so jammed with facts that it is difficult for the hapless reader to tell who did what to whom. Did the cabinet meeting kill a paratrooper? Did the paratrooper injure nine others? Who demanded Sharon's resignation? Assuming that we interpreted the sentence correctly, our revision breaks it into logical units and makes the meaning clear.)

Just for the Fun of It

Having come this far in our book, you have earned a reward. Let us therefore share with you, just for the fun of it, some nuggets mined from the daily press of America. They are not items of dubious origin, taken from some collection that, like a chain letter, has been around the world seven times. They are real. We've seen the originals.

from the *Atlanta Constitution*:
> PREMIER ANESTHESIA REPLACES CHIEF
> WITH HEAD OF PARENT

from the *Chicago Sun-Times*:
> DEAD BOY, 12, WAS DRIVING STOLEN CAR

from the *Grand Rapids Press* (Grand Rapids, Michigan):
> YOUNGSTER SHOT WHILE DRIVING
> SCHOOL BUS OUT OF HOSPITAL

from the *Daily Sentinel* (Grand Junction, Colorado):
> FRUITA MAN JAILED AFTER DROWNING

from *USA Today*:
> FAMILY FIGHTS TO KEEP GOING AFTER ANDREW

from the *Star-Ledger* (Newark, New Jersey):
> VOLUNTEERS CAN HELP RAPE VICTIMS

from the *Oakland Press* (Pontiac, Michigan):
> HONEYBAKED THIEF SOUGHT BY POLICE

from the *Daily News* (Winona, Minnesota):
> GROWE PROPOSES BROADER USE OF ABSENTEE BALLADS

from the *Democrat-Gazette* (Little Rock, Arkansas):
> LEGISLATORS TAX BRAINS TO CUT DEFICIT

from the *Rocky Mountain News* (Denver, Colorado):
> JOURNALIST FOUND DEAD WHILE
> INVESTIGATING ALLEGED THEFT

from the *Democrat-Gazette* (Little Rock, Arkansas):
> OBSERVERS SAY EXECUTION WOULD HELP CLINTON IMAGE

from the *Rocky Mountain News* (Denver, Colorado):
> COURT MAKES DEATH PENALTY RETROACTIVE

from the *Atlanta Constitution*:
> WOMAN HIT BY TRAIN IN INTENSIVE CARE

from the *Enquirer* (Columbus, Georgia):
> PRIVATES HELD IN SEXUAL ASSAULT

from the *Boston Herald*:
> EXXON VALDEZ SKIPPER ACQUITTED
> OF BEING DRUNK IN SPILL

from the *Democrat-Gazette* (Little Rock, Arkansas):
> 40 SALUTE OFFICERS KILLED IN LINE
> OF DUTY IN CAPITOL CEREMONY

Finally, early in 1992, Queen Elizabeth II, reflecting on the year just past, described 1991 as *annus horribilis*. Commenting editorially, the *Los Angeles Times* omitted one of the *n*'s from *annus*, turning Her Majesty's description of the year into a royal pain in the you-know-what.

POINTS TO PONDER AND REMEMBER

- ☛ Good syntax does not necessarily mean good writing, but bad syntax always means bad writing.
- ☛ After you have written something, read it over to make sure you have said what you meant to say. Then read it again.
- ☛ You can't write without thinking. Don't even try.
- ☛ No reader should have to read a sentence twice to get its message.
- ☛ Don't dangle your participles in public.

▫ 7 ▫

How's That Again?

A celebrity athlete touting a device designed to prevent an automobile from being stolen promises eager listeners that "The Club works where other cheap imitations fail." Some company official, if not the copywriter who wrote the radio spot or the spokesman who reads it, should realize that the statement includes the Club in the category of "cheap imitations."

A business reporter opines that two recently merged companies could cut costs by eliminating duplicity. Any dictionary will give you the meaning of *duplicity*. Perhaps the reporter doesn't own a dictionary.

A political commentator refers to a governor as "the penultimate politician." Again, the writer had only to consult a dictionary to check what evidently was an unfamiliar word.

An editorial in a large daily newspaper tells us that "Caning draws blood and can cause permanent scaring." This could be a typographical error of the kind most of us make now and then, but it is the kind of error that computer spelling checkers miss.

A headline in the student newspaper of a prestigious university warns, "University Mall No Longer Col-

LECTS UNMIXED PAPER." Surely, the University Mall would not require that paper be mixed before being collected for recycling.

A daily in a southern city headlines "A NEW CHAPTER IN THE FIGHT AGAINST LITERACY," thus striking a blow either *against* literacy or *for* illiteracy.

An important East Coast daily tells readers about a coming "SPIEDIE FEST AND BALLOON RALLY," opening the article with this incredible sentence: "The city salutes its sandwich of choice, the spiedie, a regional combination of barbecued marinated chicken, pork, lamb, plus antique cars and balloons." The same newspaper describes a home with jealousy windows and tells of a young boy who was unmercilessly teased. Whatever happened to copy editors?

The writers of these examples did not say what they meant. In much of what we read and hear, the gap between what is said and what is meant is startling. We encounter examples similar to these in newspapers from cities all across the fruited plain, in national magazines, on radio and television, in political speeches, on billboards, in sales catalogues, in instruction manuals, and even, now and then, in dictionaries. Most of the people who commit these errors are intelligent. They are lawyers, doctors, engineers, architects, executives, secretaries, scientists, administrators, teachers, accountants, and even journalists. Every one of the examples is the work of someone who is paid to write. Why do so many people have so much trouble saying what they mean? There are many reasons, but a list of common faults would surely include the following:

- disregarding principles of grammar and syntax
- using punctuation improperly or ineffectively
- failing to read and reread what is written
- relying too much on vague, abstract language
- drowning information in a sea of unnecessary words
- relying on computer spelling checkers

- failing to distinguish between homophones
- using words incorrectly
- writing without thinking

From previous chapters, you know the importance of good syntax and of fat-free writing. In this chapter, we will discuss other ways to help you say what you mean.

Grappling with Grammar

For many people, grammar is a turnoff. A mere mention of the word evokes memories of a stern-faced lady, perhaps a ruler-wielding nun, who insisted that her students memorize a lot of dreary rules. And woe to the miscreant who paused while parsing a sentence or declined the teacher's invitation to decline a noun. Such English teachers have been called "Miss Grundy," "Miss Thistlebottom," and perhaps other names better left unmentioned.

We are here to praise Miss Grundy, not to bury her, for she held at least one of the keys to good writing. So she wasn't an inspirer of young Hemingways. Maybe her insistence on precision stifled creativity, as some modern teachers claim the study of grammar does, but she knew how to craft a good sentence and she knew how to say what she meant. We cannot imagine Miss Grundy having written any of the examples above. Was there a Miss Grundy in your life? If so, her worst fault might have been that she tended to give her students the impression that the rules of grammar were worth learning for their own sake. The truth is, rules are only the means to an end. The study of grammar helps us to understand the structure of English and to use the language more effectively.

Many good writers have little knowledge of grammatical rules. They write "by ear," just as some good musicians play by ear. Even writers who know grammar write by ear in the sense that they do not turn to a grammar book or think about rules every time they write a sentence; but when the ear fails, grammar is always there to fall back on. For example, consider this sentence from a professional magazine: "Especially meant for the media, the piece will be mailed to whomever makes the mistake . . ." The writer of that sentence probably relied on the ear, assuming that the *whom* form of the personal pronoun always follows the preposition *to,* as in "to whom it may concern." A little knowledge of grammar will tell you that *whoever* is required here because it is the subject of *makes,* not the object of *to.* Because a subject requires the nominative case of the pronoun, *whoever* is the correct choice.

"Grammar is to a writer what anatomy is to a sculptor or the scales to a musician," wrote B. J. Chute. "You may loathe it, it may bore you, but nothing will replace it, and, once mastered, it will support you like a rock."

All this does not mean that you must undertake a study of grammar in order to write well. It does mean that you should develop enough sensitivity to grammatical principles so that you know when to turn to the rule book.

Road Signs for the Reader

Punctuation marks do for the reader what road signs and traffic signals do for the driver. They tell when to slow down, when to stop, and what to expect along the way. Reading a book with no punctuation would be like driving through a busy city with no signs or signals. Punctuation also defines the relationship of one sentence element to another. When we punctuate well, our writing is clearer and easier to read.

In the evolution of language, punctuation came long after writing. Early writing had none. All words ran together, forcing the reader to guess where one thought ended and another began. But readers in those days had little to read and might not have minded the inconvenience. Readers today are inundated with reading material and are impatient with anything that cannot be read easily.

To understand how punctuation can affect meaning, compare these sentences:

The General Motors assembly plant, located near Atlanta, employs hundreds of people.

The General Motors assembly plant located near Atlanta employs hundreds of people.

The sentences are identical except for their punctuation, yet their meanings are different. In the first, the phrase *located near Atlanta* is set off by commas. It is a nondefining phrase that simply gives the reader a bit of incidental information about the plant. In the second, *located near Atlanta* is not set off by commas. It is a defining phrase that tells the reader which General Motors assembly plant is being discussed. The first sentence implies that General Motors has only one assembly plant and that it, by the way, is near Atlanta. The second implies that General Motors has more than one assembly plant and that the one being discussed is the one that is near Atlanta.

Here is another pair of sentences that illustrates the point. In this example, the difference in meaning is even more subtle:

She did not accept the transfer because she wanted to earn more money.

She did not accept the transfer, because she wanted to earn more money.

Did she accept the transfer? In the first sentence, she did. The sentence tells us that she accepted the transfer for some reason other than the money. The second tells us that she did not accept the transfer and the reason was that it would not pay more money.

A dependent clause such as *because she wanted more money* ordinarily would not be preceded by a comma, but when a *because* clause follows a negative statement, a comma may be needed to make the meaning clear. When you use a dependent clause beginning with *because*, always ask yourself whether a comma would clarify the sentence. If you're unsure, turn the sentence around and put the dependent clause first. If it says what you mean to say, the comma is needed in the original version. When the *because* clause opens the sentence, it must always be set off by a comma. Thus, *Because she wanted to earn more money, she did not accept the transfer.*

Punctuation, especially commas, may be used for emphasis. For example, we might write, "In 1993, the company opened five new stores." The comma after *In 1993*, a short introductory phrase, is considered optional by many writers, but it gives a slight but unmistakable emphasis to the date, in the same way that a slight pause in speaking emphasizes what follows.

A comma inserted into a federal statute where none had existed might have changed world history. The story of that inserted comma appears in the *American Journal of International Law*, October 1940, in an article entitled "The Attorney General's Opinion on the Exchange of Destroyers for Naval Bases." Here is a summary:

Shortly before America entered World War II, Great Britain was in dire straits. The Germans were bombing London almost daily. President Franklin D. Roosevelt wanted to aid the British by sending them war materials, and he was determined to do so despite pacifist sentiments in Congress. He concocted a plan by which the United States would provide destroyers to Britain, and Britain, in exchange, would allow U.S. naval vessels to be based there. The president asked his attorney general, Robert Jackson, for an opinion on the legality of his plan. Jackson determined that the Neutrality Act of 1917 seemed to prohibit the president's plan. But knowing Roosevelt's strong desire to help Britain and, presumably, sharing that desire, he had the pertinent section of the law retyped after inserting a comma in a key sentence. The comma changed the meaning of the sentence, or at least made it ambiguous, so that the president felt justified in going ahead with his plan. To our knowledge, FDR's plan was never tested in court, probably because the opposition to helping Britain went up in the smoke of Pearl Harbor.

Punctuation is more art than science. It has few unbreakable rules. In some cases—the placement of quotation marks, for example—the rules are not even logical. So what we sometimes call rules are more like conventions, adopted by consensus to make writing consistent.

Punctuation styles and preferences vary considerably, even among the best writers and publications. The modern fashion is to use punctuation marks sparingly, especially commas. Carried to extreme, this style can result in ambiguity. Overpunctuating, on the other hand, makes writing ponderous. Our recommendations for using punctuation effectively appear in Chapters 17 and 18. They are based on the conventions embraced by many of the best writers and publications today. If you follow our recommendations, you will never be "wrong," and you can be sure that your writing will be as clear as good punctuation can make it.

Send the Right Signals

A transition is a word, a phrase, or even a sentence that prepares the reader for a change of subject, a continuation, an example, a modification of a previous statement, or an antithetic statement. Like punctuation marks, transitions make reading easier. They can slow or quicken the pace of writing. Using them well can help you say what you want to say and to say it with style and grace.

The following sentences illustrate how a transition does its work:

The company earned record profit in the fourth quarter. Profit for the year was far less than expected.

The company earned record profit in the fourth quarter. Unfortunately, profit for the year was far less than expected.

The two pairs of sentences are identical excepting the transition, *unfortunately,* that opened the second sentence of the second pair. The transition eases the reader from the good news to the bad and makes the shift less jarring.

From a simple example invented for an illustration, we go to a real one taken from a large daily newspaper. The story was about the discovery of superconducting materials, which had scientists abuzz several years ago:

Independent scientists also are enthusiastic [about the discovery]. They say the density of the electrical current passed by the new superconducting materials may be too low for some applications. And they say that the materials themselves, exotic metal oxides, are too brittle to be shaped into conventional electric wiring.

The opening sentence, or what might be called the topic sentence, of the paragraph seems to promise to tell why independent scientists are enthusiastic. The remaining sentences, however, do not fulfill the promise. Instead, they give us several negatives about the discovery. A transition is sorely needed.

The writer could have resorted to a common transition such as *however*, *nevertheless*, or *even so* at the beginning of the second sentence. A better solution would be an opening sentence something like this: "Most independent scientists are enthusiastic, but some have reservations about the discovery."

Words and phrases commonly used as transitions include *for example, in addition, to illustrate, finally, at the same time, on the other hand, previously, furthermore, in conclusion,* and *in other words*. Many of these transitions are useful, but some are overused. Your writing might sound fresher if you find alternatives to the most common ones.

Skillfully placed, transitions contribute to clarity and meaning. Overused, they make writing tiresome. Your ear and your common sense should tell you when a transition is needed.

The Words We Use

"Sticks and stones may break my bones, but words will never hurt me" is what children say to someone calling them "names." Don't believe it. Words *can* hurt. They can also heal. They have power. The words we choose and how we use them go a long way in determining whether we say what we mean.

Good writing does not require a big vocabulary, but it does require that we use words properly. Writers who are careless with words risk being misunderstood or looking foolish. The business reporter who thought *duplicity* meant duplication and the political writer who described the governor as "the penultimate politician" were in the latter category.

Words have connotations that go beyond their actual meanings. Try a little unscientific experiment. Read the following words, pausing for a few seconds after each, and allow an image to come into your mind: *thin . . . slender . . . skinny . . . underweight . . . reedy . . . svelte.* These words are closely related in meaning, but the images they evoke range widely. A young athlete might be described as slender or perhaps even reedy, but probably not skinny, thin, or underweight. *Slender* is a synonym for *svelte*, but *svelte* has a different connotation. Mark Twain wrote that the difference between the right word and the almost-right word was the difference between lightning and lightning bug. It is also the difference between *skinny* and *slender*, between *fat* and *plump*, and between *in behalf of* and *on behalf of*—differences that escape careless writers.

Our Chapters 8, 9, and 10 will help you distinguish between frequently confused pairs of words, but you should also have a usage dictionary and at least one up-to-date standard dictionary. Our list of recommended reading includes examples of both, in addition to other books that will help you say what you mean.

Don't Jargonize Your Writing

Although *jargonize* appears in dictionaries, the word itself looks suspiciously like jargon. Jargonizers love to add *-ize* to nouns and in that way change them to verbs. Although this practice has been going on for centuries and has given us many useful verbs—*criticize, apologize, burglarize*, and numerous others—it has been carried to extremes in recent years. A news release from the public relations department of a symphony orchestra tells us that the orchestra "concertizes" on tour during the summer. An official of a real estate organization once told a newspaper reporter that eliminating tax deductions for interest on home loans would "disasterize" the housing industry. Words like that ought to be trasherized.

The dictionary speaks unkindly of jargon, calling it "strange, outlandish, or barbarous language" and "obscure and often pretentious language marked by circumlocution and long words." The word comes from *jargoun*, which in Middle French meant "meaningless chatter."

The dictionary also says that jargon is "the vocabulary peculiar to a particular trade, profession, or group." In this sense, not all jargon is bad. Used properly and at the proper time, it can serve as a sort of shorthand, but we suspect that much jargon is meaningless even to the people who use it. An art studio tells us that a particular form of art is "a very accelerated mode of transport of harmonial movement that balances the personal requirement for centeredness" and that "each imprintsial pattern is ac-

companied with its conceptual mode of thought idea."
Educators write of "the absence of functional structure
coupled with stress on being different," "dynamic immo-
bility," "manifestation of behavioral problems in the af-
fective domain," and, of course, "learning situations."

Some writers seem to have a shelf stocked with words
and phrases they use when they don't want to bother with
thinking. Their shelves contain ample supplies of clichés,
jargon, and buzzwords. Some of the more advanced non-
thinkers use this Instant Buzzword Generator, origin unknown, which floated around on the business-fax network
a few years ago:

Column One	Column Two	Column Three
1. Total	1. Management	1. Options
2. Systematized	2. Monitored	2. Flexibility
3. Parallel	3. Reciprocal	3. Mobility
4. Functional	4. Digital	4. Programming
5. Responsive	5. Logic	5. Concept
6. Optical	6. Transitional	6. Time-phase
7. Synchronized	7. Incremental	7. Projection
8. Compatible	8. Third-generation	8. Enhancement
9. Balanced	9. Policy	9. Contingency
0. Integrated	0. Generational	0. Capability

Here's how it works. When you need an attention-getting
phrase, just select a three-digit number at random. Then
match each digit of your number with the corresponding
word in each column. For example, if the number you
choose is 594, your buzzword phrase is "responsive policy
programming." Neat, huh? How about 833—"compatible
reciprocal mobility"? Properly used, this device can give
your writing "178"—whatever that might mean.

Physicians, lawyers, engineers, educators, and other
professionals have their own special ways of speaking and
writing. As long as they're talking with others of their
persuasion, there is no problem. Many professionals,
though, must communicate with the public, and therein

lies the rub. When jargon spills over into general usage, the risk of being misunderstood is great.

One reason for the popularity of jargon may be that it sets members of a particular group apart from the uninformed masses. Conducting a writing seminar on an army base, a teacher chided a participant, a colonel, for too much use of military jargon. "You mean," the colonel asked, "that you expect me to write like an enlisted man?" We never heard whether the colonel persevered in his battle with the teacher or whether he "executed a strategic movement to the rear," as the Macedonian king Antigonus Gonatas is said to have described his retreat more than two millennia ago.

One of our favorite anecdotes about the use of jargon comes from the soft-drink industry. In that industry, the word *sample* is often used as a verb meaning "to give out samples." Thus, sampling customers in a supermarket means to give out samples of a product. One summer, the Coca-Cola Company was urging its bottlers to hold clinics for high school students who aspired to become cheerleaders. A writer whose job was to prepare materials for bottlers to use opened a promotional brochure with this unforgettable sentence: "Bottlers will have an opportunity this summer to sample impressionable young teenagers." Is that really what the writer meant to say?

Use jargon when it suits your purpose, but remember that the indiscriminate use of jargon is the lazy way to write. Never use jargon where there is a possibility that it will mean different things to different people.

The Language of Control

A young man applying for a job was asked what salary he would expect to receive if he should be offered the job. "Well," he said, trying to sound experienced beyond his years, "I haven't decided on an exact amount, but it would

have to be in the five-figure range." The executive conducting the interview said, "I think we could manage that, but
tell me this: Are you thinking of $10,000, or do you have
in mind something closer to $99,999?"

We're probably correct in assuming that the young man
had heard the expression *five-figure income* and thought it
sounded "cool." Using it in response to the interviewer's
question made him look foolish.

You cannot communicate precisely without using specific, concrete language. If someone says to you, "It was
very cold in my hometown on New Year's Day," you must
guess what the person means by "very cold." To a person
from South Carolina, "very cold" might be, say, twenty
degrees. Someone from northern Minnesota probably
would mean *minus* twenty. Cold and hot are relative terms.
By themselves they have no precise meaning.

We call concrete language "the language of control" because its use ensures that the writer or speaker controls
the message. Nonspecific language cedes control of the
message to the reader or listener.

Concrete language is *ex*clusive; it excludes more than it
*in*cludes. Abstract language is *in*clusive; it includes more
than it *ex*cludes. Words such as *thing*, *item*, and *entity* are
abstract because they include almost everything. *You* is
concrete because it excludes everything and everybody except you. *A dozen* is concrete; *a few* is abstract. *Ten years old*
is concrete; *young* is abstract. *She can play "Maple Leaf Rag"*
on the piano is concrete; *She is an accomplished musician*
is abstract.

How about the word *machine*? Is it concrete or abstract?
The answer is "yes." That is, it's a bit of both. A machine
can be a vacuum cleaner, a cotton gin, a computer, a den-
tist's drill, or an aircraft; but an apple, a rock, a dog, or a
house is not a machine. So *machine* both includes and excludes. Of the machines mentioned, consider *aircraft*. It
is more concrete than *machine*, but it, too, includes and

excludes. It includes helicopters, seaplanes, gliders, and jet planes. You can see where this is leading: A jet can be a fighter, bomber, or an airliner. An airliner can be a DC 10, an L1011, or a 747. Can anything be more concrete than 747? Yes. Try Delta 747, or Delta 747 serial number so-and-so, or the Delta 747 that at this moment is landing at Los Angeles International Airport.

The more concrete the word, the more precise its meaning. Good writing does not mean always using concrete words. You, the writer, must decide what degree of precision is required for the subject. You must understand the effect that generalities, or nonspecific language, have on what you write. To dramatize that effect, we want to introduce you to our friend Senator Pfillmore Pfogbottom:

Senator Pfillmore Pfogbottom is a veteran of the United States Senate. Last November, he was reelected by an overwhelming majority. He is not a wealthy man, but before his election to the Senate, he earned a comfortable living as a lawyer. His wife, Pfanny Pfae Pfogbottom, is an executive who commands a salary well into five figures.

The senator is known throughout official Washington as an unparalleled raconteur on the Senate floor and an enthusiastic roué in his off-duty time. He also plays golf, but he does not play as often as he would like to play. He is considered a very good golfer for one who plays so seldom.

Senator and Mrs. Pfogbottom have two children, Pfineas and Pfyllis. Pfineas plays basketball on his high school team, and the coach describes him as "a scrappy player and a valuable member of the team despite the fact that he is of only average height." Pfyllis loves to read and usually reads several books a month. She is, however, addicted to "trashy" novels. Her parents admit she isn't a "brain," but they insist she is an above-average student.

Senator Pfogbottom once introduced a bill related to the exportation of freezers to Siberia. It was defeated decisively.

TEST YOURSELF

Answer the following questions about Senator Pfogbottom. Circle one, but only one, choice for each question. Look back as often as you like.

1. How long has Pfogbottom been a Senator?
   (a) 5 years   **(b)** 10 years   **(c)** 25 years
2. What percentage of the vote did he receive last November?
   (a) 51%   **(b)** 60%   **(c)** 80%
3. What is the senator's net worth?
   (a) $100,000   **(b)** $1,000,000   **(c)** $1.98
4. How much did he earn as a lawyer?
   (a) $15,000 a year   **(b)** $50,000 a year   **(c)** $400 an hour
5. What is Pfanny's salary?
   (a) $10,000   **(b)** $50,000   **(c)** $100,000 plus tips
6. What is a typical golf score for the senator?
   (a) 72   **(b)** 90   **(c)** 132   **(d)** Depends on who's counting
7. How tall is Pfineas?
   (a) 5 feet, 7 inches   **(b)** 6 feet   **(c)** 3 meters
8. How many books does Pfyllis read each month?
   (a) three   **(b)** ten   **(c)** twenty
9. What is her grade average?
   (a) A-minus   **(b)** B-plus   **(c)** C   **(d)** C-plus
10. Was the senator for or against exporting freezers to Siberia?
    (a) For   **(b)** Against
11. How many votes did his proposal receive?
    (a) 40   **(b)** 20   **(c)** 3   **(d)** Only his
12. Why am I doing this, anyway?
    (a) Because Lederer and Dowis asked me to
    (b) Pfor pfun

Think, Think, Think

For many years, IBM used a memorable one-word slogan—*THINK*. Little signs bearing the word were posted at employees' work stations. The company even published a magazine called *THINK*. What good advice! Much bad writing could be prevented if writers would heed it. When writers fail to say what they mean, it's often because they don't think.

A memorandum from the U.S. Fish and Wildlife Service contained this statement: "[Duck] eggs eaten by predators have an unacceptably low likelihood of hatching." Do tell.

An article in the British medical journal *Lancet* claimed that "Sudden death, though rare, is frequent." We're thankful for that. Maybe.

When the great soprano Roberta Peters took ill and had to cancel a concert, the concert promoter sent a message saying that Ms. Peters "was taken by a raging head cold which makes it impossible for her to sing or fly." Fly? Mary Martin as Peter Pan, maybe. Roberta Peters as Carmen, nahhhh!

In a paper on Shakespeare's *Othello*, a student wrote: "Soon Yahoo starts to cast aspersions on Testimonial's chastity." The teacher surmised that the student's computer spelling checker was unable to recognize *Iago* and *Desdemona* and suggested *yahoo* and *testimonial* as alternatives. The student let the computer do the thinking. Spelling checkers are useful, but they are only mechanical devices. They are a poor substitute for the human brain.

Good writing is often so direct, so simple, that it almost seems as if the writer just "dashed it off" without thinking. William Butler Yeats wrote:

> *A line will take us hours, may be;*
> *Yet if it does not seem a moment's thought,*
> *Our stitching and unstitching has been naught.*

Yeats was writing poetry about poetry, but the principle applies to any kind of writing. If something sounds as if it was easy to write, it probably wasn't.

Writing and thinking are inseparable. Not only does thinking help us to write, writing helps us to think.

POINTS TO PONDER AND REMEMBER

- ☛ Grammar helps us to understand how English is structured and to learn to use the language better.
- ☛ Punctuation is more art than science; it has few unbreakable rules.
- ☛ Think before you write. After you have written, think about what you have written.

□ 8 □

Troublesome Twins

Writing is, above all, a craft. True craftsmen and crafts-women know how to use the tools of their craft to create something beautiful and useful from raw material. Ideas and information are the raw materials writers begin with, words their tools. Employing words effectively means us-ing them with as much precision and pride as possible.

In *The Reader over Your Shoulder*, Robert Graves and Alan Hodges advised:

> No writer of English can be sure of using exactly the right words, even in a simple context, and even after twenty or thirty years of self-education. But he should at least act on the assumption that, . . . though he may not always find [exactly] the right word, he can at least learn by experience to avoid the quite wrong, and even the not quite wrong ones.

Avoiding the "quite wrong" words—and choosing right words—is what this chapter and the next two are about. Earlier we touched briefly on word usage. That discussion now continues with a concise lexicon of words that are most often used incorrectly. As the *United Press Interna-tional Stylebook* cautions, "A burro is an ass. A burrow is a hole in the ground. As a [writer] you are expected to know the difference."

But why should we care about such differences, some

ask, when the message is clear? It is true that everyone understands the supermarket signs that mark checkout lanes by proclaiming "8 Items or Less," rather than "8 Items or Fewer." Granted, we know what "between you and I" means. Sure, when people say, "I ain't in the mood for no potatoes," we don't pass them the potatoes.

But language does more than transfer ideas. It also conveys impressions. Language is part of your behavior, just like your manners, habits of dress, and general conduct. You jump into dungarees and an old T-shirt before dashing off on a hayride, but you don't wear such an outfit to most houses of worship. You don a tuxedo or long gown for a formal dance but not for workaday occasions. Dining at home, you may pick up a chop with your fingers, but at most restaurants you use a knife and fork.

So it is with language. When you are among educated people, you must employ the dialect appropriate to the situation. Using nonstandard or careless words, expressions, and structures is like saying, "Good morning, Joseph" to your best friend Joe or "How's it hangin', Frankie?" to your clergyman.

The word *communicate* comprises two Latin roots that mean "with" and "obligation." The most important function of language is communication, which carries an obligation to make clear contact with other human beings. Robert Pooley has justly defined good grammar as "that language that creates the least discomfort among the largest number of participants." Inappropriate diction crackles static through any message you are trying to communicate.

Our English language has acquired the largest vocabulary of all the world's languages, at least three times as many words as the lexicon of any other. No wonder, then, that so many troublesome twins (and an occasional triplet) teem our tongues and dot our dictionaries. Here is a quick-reference guide to fifty of the most confusing:

accept / except

Which students received a special exemption?:

a. The draft board accepted the students.
b. The draft board excepted the students.

The answer is the second group of students. *Except* can be a verb that means "to leave out from a whole" or a preposition that means "with the exception of":

One day, women may no longer be *excepted* from fighting on the front lines.

The museum is open daily, *except* Sundays.

Accept, a verb that sounds much like *except*, means "to receive with approval":

The eighty-year-old great-grandmother proudly *accepted* the high school diploma she had just earned.

adapt / adopt

Which leader is more resourceful?:

a. The mayor adapted her predecessor's policies.
b. The mayor adopted her predecessor's policies.

The answer is the first mayor, who shaped her predecessor's policies to her own ends. *Adapt* is a verb that means "to adjust or make suitable." *Adopt* means "to take as one's own":

Her eyes soon *adapted* to the harsh light.

Most of Eugene O'Neill's plays have been *adapted* for television.

Many adolescents *adopt* the air of world-weary old men and women.

adverse / averse

Something *adverse* is unfavorable. *Averse*, always followed by the preposition *to*, is an adjective meaning "to be opposed":

We may be *averse* to tax increases because we believe that they create *adverse* business conditions.

aggravate / annoy / irritate

To *aggravate* something is to make it worse; to *annoy* and to *irritate* mean "to bother, to disturb":

He was *annoyed* when he received the check three weeks late. The fact that it was for the wrong amount *aggravated* the situation.

alternate / alternative

An *alternate*, as a noun, is one who is empowered to act for another. Usually, *alternate* is an adjective or verb. It is not interchangeable with *alternative*, which is a noun that means "another choice." Strictly speaking, that choice should be between two possibilities, but most writers today use *alternative* even when the choice is among several:

His moods *alternate* between black rage and soaring ecstasy.

Greta was elected as an *alternate* student council senator.

Unless the world gains control of its population growth, I see no *alternative* but widespread famine.

amount / number

Use *number* to refer to persons or things that can be counted. Use *amount* to refer to quantities. *Number* tells how many; *amount* tells how much:

Rocco made a great *amount* of money selling a large *number* of tickets to the new freshmen granting them permission to use the toilets.

anxious / eager

To be *anxious* is to be worried; to be *eager* is to anticipate with keen interest or enthusiasm:

We hope that you are *eager* to learn more about English usage—and not too *anxious* about the subject.

appraise / apprise

When we *appraise*, we evaluate; when we *apprise*, we inform. The verb *apprise* is always followed by the preposition *of*:

We were *apprised* of the fact that an insurance representative would soon arrive to *appraise* the damage wrought by the fire.

assure / ensure / insure

To *assure* is to promise something to someone. To *ensure* is to make certain. To *insure* is to safeguard. Bergen and Cornelia Evans offer an excellent illustration of how these words differ:

To be well *insured ensures* peace of mind and is vastly *assuring*.

awhile / a while

Awhile is an adverb meaning "for a time." Use *a while*, not *awhile*, as an object of the preposition *for*:

Stay *awhile* and let us talk of cabbages and kings for *a while*.

beside / besides

Which speaker is smarter?:

a. In the room were four geniuses beside me.
b. In the room were four geniuses besides me.

The answer is the second speaker. "Besides me" means that the speaker, in addition to four others, is a genius.

Beside is most commonly used to mean "by the side of." *Besides* means "in addition to" or "except" or, as an adverb, "moreover":

She ate nothing *besides* a piece of toast.

There is really only enough for two; *besides*, Sally doesn't like to eat giant squid.

I sat *beside* Merriwether, whose remark was completely *beside* the point.

borrow / lend

We use *borrow* when we mean "to get something from another with the understanding that it must be returned." We use *lend* when we mean "let another have or use for a time":

Although Irving has *borrowed* my eraser and forgotten to return it, I agreed to *lend* him my gallon jug of Liquid Paper.

bring / take

Which request would parents be more likely to make of their children?:

a. Take the stray dog home.
b. Bring the stray dog home.

Parents would probably prefer that the stray mutt travel

in a direction away from their home. Hence, they would be more likely to make the first request.

The verb *bring* suggests motion toward the speaker. The verb *take* suggests motion away from the speaker. We bring in the newspaper; we take out the trash:

> *Take* this note to Valdez, and *bring* me his answer this afternoon.

We long for the revival of the almost moribund verb *fetch*, which means "to go and get and bring back":

> At 3:00 P.M. I must fetch our daughter from school.

can / may

Can applies to what is possible, *may* to what is permissible. "Can I get a drink of water, teacher?" many a student has asked. Of course. Just about everyone is *able* to get a drink of water. The question is "May I [have permission to] get a drink of water?"

capital / capitol

Capitol comes down to us from the Capitolium, an ancient Roman temple dedicated to the worship of Jupiter. *Capitol* refers either to the Capitol building in Washington, D.C., which is always capitalized (the pun is unavoidable) or a building in which a state legislature meets. The *capital* of a state or nation is the city in which the *capitol* is located—i.e., the seat of government.

compare to / compare with

Use *compare to* when relating things that are dissimilar. Use *compare with* when discussing things in the same category:

Compared with its performance last year, the Slime Shampoo Company is doing well.

Shall I *compare* thee *to* a summer's day?

complement / compliment

Which twosome is playing doubles?:

a. Ellen complimented Frank's tennis game.
b. Ellen complemented Frank's tennis game.

The answer is the twosome in the second sentence.

Because *compliment* and *complement* sound alike, they cannot be misused in speaking. They are, however, often confused in writing. *Compliment*, as a noun or verb, involves an expression of admiration. *Complement*, as a noun or verb, involves something that completes. A helpful mnemonic device is to visualize *complement* as *comple(te)ment*:

Her precision of speech drew many *compliments*.

As your best friend, I *compliment* you on your taste in people.

The flaming dessert was a perfect *complement* to a fine meal.

The polka-dotted sash *complemented* the raging stripes of her dress.

conscience / conscientious / conscious

To sort out these troublesome triplets: Your *conscience* is your sense of obligation to do right. When you are *conscientious*, you conform to the dictates of conscience. When you are *conscious*, you are aware:

Our *conscience* distinguishes us from the brutes.

Our *conscientious* scoutmaster wove a lanyard six yards long.

I became *conscious* that people were staring at a piece of macaroni hanging from my nose.

continual / continuous

Continual means "repetitive." *Continuous* means "unbroken." A telephone may ring continually but not continuously. The pollution of our planet appears, alas, to be continuous, not just continual.

convince / persuade

These words are often used interchangeably, but the distinction between them is worth preserving. To *convince* someone means to bring that person to your point of view. To *persuade* someone is to induce that person to do something. *Convince* is usually followed by *of* or *that*. *Persuade* is usually followed by an infinitive (*to* plus a verb):

I am *convinced* of your ability to sort out confusing word pairs.

They *convinced* me that I should resign immediately.

I trust that I have *persuaded* you to preserve the distinction between *convince* and *persuade*.

discreet / discrete

These homophones are quite different in meaning. *Discreet* means "prudent," while *discrete* means "separate":

It was *discreet* of Mabel not to mention to the boss that Irving can't sleep without having his pink dinosaur doll on his pillow.

Discreet and *discrete* are two *discrete* entities.

emigrate / immigrate

Like *bring* and *take*, the distinction has to do with direction. *Emigrants* or *émigrés* depart from a country, permanently, in order to *immigrate* to another country and become *immigrants*.

enormity / emormousness

Enormousness refers to great size, either physical or figurative. An *enormity* is something that is monstrous or apalling. Thus, we may speak of the *enormity* of Stalin's crimes, but we should refer to the *enormousness* of the former Soviet Union.

figuratively / literally

We hope that you are keeping your eyes glued to this page, but only figuratively glued. If your eyes were literally epoxied to this text, you would be ocularly challenged and wouldn't be able to read a word we've written. In fact, the chances of that happening are about as small as the chances of your literally rolling in the aisles while watching a funny movie or literally drowning in tears while watching a sad one. Don't use *literally*, "by the letter; strictly construed," when you mean *figuratively*, "so to speak."

flaunt / flout

In which of the following statements is Horace cashing in on his father's power?:

a. Horace flaunts his father's authority.
b. Horace flouts his father's authority.

The answer is the first statement. *Flaunt* is a verb that means "to make a display of." *Flout* is another verb that means "to ignore contemptuously." Thus, conspicuous consumption is *flaunting* one's wealth, while reckless driving is *flouting* the traffic laws.

flotsam / jetsam

When used together, as they often are, these two terms are not simply redundancies. After a shipwreck, *flotsam* is the stuff found *floating* on the water; *jetsam* is the stuff that has been thrown overboard—*jettisoned*. For you as a writer this may be the least useful piece of information in this chapter, but it may come in handy one day when you are paddling through one identifiable kind of wreckage.

forego / forgo

To *forgo* is to give up or do without. *Forgo* is often confused with *forego*, which means "to go before." *Forego*, used correctly, is rare, but its present and past participles, *foregoing* and *foregone*, are common.

foreword / forward

A *foreword* is what its word parts indicate—a brief comment at the beginning ("fore") of a book about the purpose of that book. Although the front matter may make you look forward to reading the text, a *foreword* is not a *forward*.

formally / formerly

Which pair had met previously?:

a. We were formally introduced.
b. We were formerly introduced.

The answer is the pair in the second statement. The adverb *formally* has to do with manner; it answers the question "how?" The adverb *formerly* has to do with time; it answers the question "when?":

In all the glitter of the party, I was never *formally* introduced to Lord Bulgebottom.

He was *formerly* a bulb-changer for lighthouses before technology made him obsolete.

hanged / hung

In formal (but not just former) English, people, alas, are *hanged* and pictures and things are *hung*. When we use the verb *hang* to refer to acts of execution or suicide, the principal parts of the verb are: *hang* (present tense), *hanged* (past tense), and *hanged* (present perfect tense).

In all other contexts, the principal parts of the verb are *hang* (present tense), *hung* (past tense), *hung* (present perfect tense):

They *hanged* Short John Silverstein from the yardarm.

Over the mantel he *hung* the picture of the slathering vampire.

have / of

The helping verb *have* and its contraction *'ve* sound like *of* in rapid speech. But avoid writing *of* for *have* or *'ve*:

We should *have* predicted that the bottom would drop out of real estate.

As a cake-lover, I would*'ve* enjoyed meeting Marie Antoinette.

healthful / healthy

Something that is *healthful* causes us to feel *healthy*:

His doctor recommended that, to become more *healthy,* he should move to the *healthful* environment of the country.

home / hone

Some writers use *honing in* on something when they mean *homing in*. *Hone* means "to sharpen," so one can't hone in on anything:

You can *hone* your writing skills by *homing* in on confusing word pairs.

incredible / incredulous

When something is *incredible*, it's unbelievable. When people are *incredulous*, they are unbelieving or skeptical:

Thea's ability to master foreign languages is *incredible*.

We were *incredulous* when she told us that she had mastered Swahili in a single summer of study.

lectern / podium

Senator Mudslinger is walking up onto the *podium*. Now he stands upon a *podium* and puts his notes on the *podium*.

What goes here? Can a podium be a stage, a small base, and a slant-topped desk behind which speakers stand and on which they place their notes?

Apparently, a podium can be all these things, but for discriminating writers, a *lectern* (from the Latin *lectura*, "to read") is the slant-topped desk, a *podium* (from the Greek *podia*, "foot") the small base. The whole stage is a *platform*, *dais*, or *rostrum*.

let / leave

The verb *let*—not the verb *leave*—means "allow or permit." *Leave* means "to go away" or "not to take something with you":

His father wouldn't *let* him play video games on the family spreadsheet.

Don't *leave* your salamanders in my purse.

loose / lose

Which Hood was careless?

a. In tight situations, Robin Hood tended to lose arrows.
b. In tight situations, Robin Hood tended to loose arrows.

The answer is that, misplacing his weapons, the first Hood was careless.

Loose, most commonly an adjective that means "relaxed," occasionally appears as a verb meaning "to let loose." That may be why *loose* is occasionally confused with the verb *lose*, which means "to miss from one's possession":

Be sure not to *lose* your Junior Woody Woodsman badge.

The angry woman *loosed* a barrage of allegations against the alligators.

may / might

Grammatically, there is no difference between *may* and *might* when they're used to express uncertainty. Most of the time the two are interchangeable. To the sensitive ear, however, *might* conveys a greater degree of uncertainty, *may* a stronger degree of possibility:

If you read this book, you *may* learn to write better, and you *might* even earn more money.

nauseated / nauseous

Something that is poisonous makes you poisoned. Thus, if you say, "I'm nauseous today," some wiseacre might shoot back, "How honest of you to admit that!" The problem with this logic is that the agent that makes one feel nauseated must itself be nauseous, as in "The nauseous fumes made me nauseated," and that use of *nauseous* would bewilder most readers. Still, if you must get sick in front of a grammar purist, please feel nauseated, rather than nauseous.

noisome / noisy

Noisome has nothing to do with noise. The word is formed from a shortening of *annoy* and the adjective suffix *-some*. Most frequently, *noisome* describes an offensive odor, annoying to the point of being nauseous, or at least nauseating.

oral / verbal

Oral refers to the mouth. Therefore, oral communication is speech. *Verbal* refers to words. Therefore, verbal communication is communication that uses words, whether the words are written or spoken. In this sense, the famous line attributed to the late movie mogul Sam Goldwyn, "A verbal contract isn't worth the paper it's written on," isn't so funny after all.

In common usage, however, *verbal* has come to mean *oral*. When people tell you that they have "a verbal contract," rather than asking, "Is that oral or written?" you can bet they have nothing in writing.

penultimate / ultimate

These two adjectives are not synonyms. Something *penultimate* is next-to-last, nothing more. It carries no connotation of superiority. Something *ultimate* is last and often suggests superiority, as in "the ultimate in men's clothing."

A naval commander representing the U.S. Defense Department once exulted, "In Star Wars, America has finally come up with the penultimate defense system!" Gulp. Gasp. The last thing we want is a penultimate system of national defense.

The speaker obviously thought that *penultimate* means "the absolute ultimate." So do a lot of other folks, including one Tony Award winner who gushed, "I knew what my goal was when I saw Lauren Bacall touring in a play in Buffalo. To be an actress like that—well, to me that was the penultimate!"

Penultimate doesn't mean "the absolute ultimate." Nothing can be more than ultimate.

pore / pour

Although we occasionally encounter a carelessly written sentence in which someone "pours" over a book (glug, glug goes the ginger ale all over the text), *pour* means "to cause liquid to flow," while *pore*, as a verb, means "to read thoroughly":

> She *poured* the catsup generously over the green eggs and ham while, desperate to find a job, she *pored* over the want ads.

precede / proceed

We use *precede* to mean "to go before" and *proceed* to mean "to go on or forward":

> *Preceding* the main speaker, she *proceeded* to outline the events for the day.

preventive / preventative

Preventive, especially as an adjective, is the preferred form. That's why the impeccable Henry W. Fowler, in *Mod-*

ern English Usage, remarks that "*preventative* is a needless lengthening of an established word, due to oversight and caprice." That's why a Secretary of Health and Welfare once cautioned that "aspirin is not a substitute for other preventive therapies for heart attack."

principal / principle

Which town probably has the stronger school system?

a. I admire the town's principles.
b. I admire the town's principals.

The answer is the second town, although it's close because both principles and principals are important to education. Before we confuse you further, read on.

Despite the existence of a well-known memory jogger ("the principal is your pal"), these two words are often confused. *Principal* can be used as a noun or as an adjective, both meaning "chief." *Principle* is a noun meaning "fundamental law or truth":

> The *principal* belief of the high school *principal* was the *principle* that every student was capable of achieving success.

prone / supine

Which person can see the sky?:

a. The camper lay prone on the grass.
b. The camper lay supine on the grass.

The answer is the second camper. Medical folk know that one who is *prone* lies face down while one who is *supine* lies face up. Careful writers adhere to the same distinction. A useful mnemonic device is that one who is supine is lying on his or her spine:

> He lay *supine* on the table while the masseur kneaded his face.

He lay *prone* on the table while the masseur kneaded his back.

Prone can also be defined as "having a tendency or inclination," a second meaning that allows John Simon to pun wryly, "When it comes to learning good English, most people are prone to be supine." Nowadays, *supine* is a rare word, while *prone* has come to signify all manner of reclining. Thus, a U.S. senator once declaimed, "In the 1930s, we were not just a nation on our backs. We were prone on our backs." We trust that in the wake of the foregoing (not forgoing) explanation of the differences between *prone* and *supine*, the absurdity of the senator's statement is clear.

sewage / sewerage

Sewerage is a system for disposing of *sewage*. If you need an adjective, use *sewage*:

The city is improving our *sewerage* by installing many new *sewage* lines.

stanch / staunch

What a difference a small internal sound change can make. Normal horses *champ*, not *chomp*, at the bit to arrive at their *stamping*, not *stomping*, grounds. In the same way, we *stanch* ("stop"), not *staunch*, the flow of blood. Of these distinctions we remain *staunch* ("loyal, steadfast") supporters.

wet / whet

Whet means "to sharpen," while its near-homophone, *wet*, means "to moisten." Thus, when we read ads that boast, "our menu will wet your appetite," we want to shout, "Great expectorations!"

Beth's success in stained glass served to *whet* her desire to become a glass blower.

The boys invaded the whistle factory and, hurling water balloons and squirting mega–water pistols, managed to *wet* every single whistle.

TEST YOURSELF

The abundance of words in English yields sets that are similar in sound, meaning, and structure and are, therefore, frequently confused. To discover how a slight difference in appearance can make a vast difference in meaning and effect, try your skill at the following quiz. Choose the correct italicized word in each sentence:

1. Some people in high places are not *adverse/averse* to accepting bribes.

2. A great *amount/number* of health plans are distributing information about *preventative/preventive* medicine.

3. My pet Gila monster always walks obediently *beside/besides* me.

4. *Bring/take* the ice sculpture from this table to the steam bath.

5. I *complemented/complimented* Jones on how his tie *complemented/complimented* his suit.

6. He liked his job except for the *continual/continuous* travel.

7. Some taxpayers *flaunt/flout* the law by submitting inaccurate returns.

8. She chose to *forego/forgo* any reward for her heroism.

9. She *preceded/proceeded* to tell her side of the story, effectively *stanching/staunching* the flow of questions from reporters.

10. We wrote this book with the *principal/principle* that effective writing is a craft as well as an art.

ANSWERS
---

1. averse 2. number, preventive 3. beside 4. Take
5. complimented, complemented 6. continual 7. flout
8. forgo 9. proceeded, stanching 10. principle

□ 9 □

The Terrible Ten

Which baseball player has wings?:

a. The batter flied out to left field.
b. The batter flew out to left field.

Which dog is definitely not a bloodhound?:

a. The dog smelled bad.
b. The dog smelled badly.

Which speaker is more likely to be a magician?:

a. She embellished her talk with a number of allusions.
b. She embellished her talk with a number of illusions.

Which child is afflicted with a defect?:

a. Maggie went shopping with her tow-headed son.
b. Maggie went shopping with her toe-headed son.

The answer to each question is the second sentence. As these distinctions indicate, word choice is not just a matter of diction. Word choice affects meaning.

If you say or write, "The book is laying on the table," you can be certain that everyone will understand what you mean, even though you will not be correct according to

131

accepted rules. If you say or write, "The hen is laying on the table," your listener or reader will not know whether the fowl is prostrate on the table or producing an egg there. To understand the difference, you need to know that *lay* is almost always a transitive verb that takes an object. A book cannot lay anything, being physiologically unsuited for a task that the hen accomplishes with ease.

Here are ten confusables that you are most likely to hear and read. Our experience as writers and teachers tells us that these particular twins often produce the most perplexing and egregious errors:

affect / effect

Affect, beginning with an *a*, is almost always a verb meaning "to have an effect on; to move or stir the emotions of":

The music of Beethoven always seems to *affect* me powerfully.

Affect is sometimes confused with another verb, *effect*, which means "to bring about":

Dean Throckmorton plans to *effect* drastic changes in the college's disciplinary system.

Effect may also be used as a noun that means "a result, an outcome":

President Abraham Lincoln's three-minute address at Gettysburg has had an enduring *effect* on the American sense of nationhood.

The most common confusion is to spell the noun *effect* as *affect*. Do not try the following sentence at home, or anywhere else:

The computer has a powerful *affect* on the speed of communication.

among / between

Use *between* ("by twain") when discussing relationships between two persons or things. Generally use *among* when discussing more than two:

> Uncle divided the Gunky Bar *between* Sam and me and then distributed the Robo-Accountant toys *among* us five boys.

When you write about more than two entities and you want to stress that each is individually related to the others, *between* may be the better choice:

> What is the difference *between* football, soccer, and rugby?

> The president has proposed a treaty *between* the United States, Canada, and Mexico.

compose / comprise

Comprise means "to include, contain, or embrace." The whole *comprises* the parts, and the parts *compose* the whole. "Is comprised of" is clunky because "is included of" and "is contained of" make no sense.

The Union *comprises* the fifty states, or the Union *is composed of* fifty states, but the Union cannot be comprised of the fifty states, nor do the fifty states comprise the Union.

Some readers would raise eyebrows and wag fingers at this sentence in a popular novel: "Ten brightly colored floats comprised the heart of the parade, although mechanical problems frequently reduced the number of entries by half." But this sentence in a recent newspaper editorial passes muster: "Our board of contributors, now in its seventh year, comprises 15 to 20 local writers with something to say about local life."

Before you blur the *comprise/compose* distinction, know your listeners and readers. If that audience comprises the dwindling few who comprehend and actually adhere to the difference, don't compromise *comprise*.

different from / different than

Than is ordinarily used with comparative adjectives, such as *better than* and *stronger than*—but *different* is not a comparative. Although *different than* is commonly used in informal speech, careful writers prefer *different from* before a noun, pronoun, or noun expression:

His political philosophy is *different from* mine.

Today's computers are *different from* those of even a few years ago.

Different than is the most common form that introduces an adverbial clause (statement containing a subject and verb) of comparison:

Returning many years later, she found that her home town was *different than* she remembered it.

The meaning of the word *reek* is *different than* it was in Shakespeare's time.

disinterested / uninterested

Which judge would you prefer?:

a. At the trial the judge was completely uninterested.
b. At the trial the judge was completely disinterested.

The answer is that you would prefer the second judge. To be *disinterested* is to be impartial. To be *uninterested* is to be unconcerned. At your trial you want a judge who is disinterested, but not uninterested.

farther / further

Use *farther* for concrete, physical distance, *further* for abstract, metaphoric distance. *Farther* means "physically beyond"; *further* means "additional" or "additionally." The choice is not always clear-cut—"let's go one step farther with this idea" versus "let's go one step further with this idea"—but careful writers make the distinction most of the time:

> At times, Uranus is *farther* from the sun than is Pluto.

> The committee members requested *further* details about the national health plan so that they could *further* explore its consequences.

fewer / less

We see them everywhere—the plague of plaques in supermarket express lines that say, "8 Items or Less." They should read, "8 Items or Fewer."

Less means "not so much" and refers to amount or quantity. *Fewer* means "not so many" and refers to number, things that are countable—"less food" but "fewer cookies"; "less nutrition" but (no matter what those over-the-hill jocks say on the Miller Lite commercials) "fewer calories." With those omnipresent supermarket signs and with those contests asking for responses in "twenty-five words or less," when will we ever learn?

imply / infer

Use *imply* to mean "indicate without saying outright" or "express indirectly." Use *infer* to mean "draw a conclusion by reasoning":

> His tone *implied* that he did not really believe us.

> We *inferred* from his tone that he thought we were lying.

Which statement definitely contains two people?:

a. Mary implied that she was unhappy with the job.
b. Mary inferred that she was unhappy with the job.

The answer is the second sentence. For Mary to "draw a conclusion" that she was unhappy with the job, "Mary" and "she" must be two different people.

lay / lie

Caveat Scriptor—Writer Beware: more than any of the other troublesome twins, these verbs lie in wait ready to lay confusion and embarrassment upon you.

In a *Hagar the Horrible* comic strip, the portly Viking and his trusty sidekick Eddie are walking along a road past four signs, one after the other, that read: "Death and Demons" . . . "Lay Ahead" . . . "If You Don't Turn Back" . . . "You'll Lose Your Head."

Before we mercilessly lay blame on Hagar for blurring the boundaries between *lie* and *lay*, we should note that these two verbs may be the most frequently confused pair in the English language. Here's the problem: *Lie* is a strong, irregular verb that conjugates *lie, lay, lain. Lay* is a weak, regular verb that conjugates *lay, laid, laid.* Because *lay* is both the present tense of *to lay* and the past tense of *to lie* and because the weak, regular verb pattern has become dominant in English, many speakers and writers use *lay*— as in "I like to lay in my hammock" (quite a trick!)—when they should use *lie.*

The most useful way to sort out *lie* and *lay* is to bear in mind that *lie* is an intransitive verb that means "to repose," while *lay* is usually a transitive verb that means "to put." *Lay* almost always takes an object, *lie* never. Something must be laid, and nothing can be lied. Or try visualizing this cartoon: Two hens are pictured side by side in their nests. One is sitting upright, and she is labeled LAYING; the other is flat on her back and labeled LYING. In another bestial cartoon, a man says to his dog, "Lay down!" and the dog rolls over on its back. Then the master says, "Speak!"—and the dog says, "It's *lie.*"

Test Yourself

Now it's time to lay your knowledge on the line. In each sentence below provide the proper form of *lie* or *lay*:

1. The workers are _____ linoleum in the kitchen.
2. I'm tired and would like to _____ down.
3. Now I _____ me down to sleep.
4. We found a man _____ in a ditch.
5. She had just _____ down to rest when the telephone rang.
6. For months he _____ in a deep coma.
7. I see that you have finally _____ your cards on the table.
8. She _____ the work aside for a few days.
9. The book is _____ on the oak table in the study.
10. For three days, the book has _____ on the shelf.

--- ANSWERS ---

| 1. laying | 2. lie | 3. lay | 4. lying | 5. lain |
| 6. lay | 7. laid | 8. laid | 9. lying | 10. lain |

unique / *unusual*

Until recently, *unique* did not possess a comparative or superlative form; something either was unique, "one of a kind," or it wasn't. Nowadays we hear and see *unique* compared (*more, most*) intensified (*very, quite*), or qualified (*rather, somewhat*).

President Reagan praised the United Way as "a very unique opportunity to serve our local communities," and Illinois governor James Thompson called a particular case "the most unique and difficult" one that had ever come before him.

Clearly, *unique* is taking on a second meaning, "unusual," to stand alongside its older meaning, "unequaled."

In fact, this upstart meaning threatens to swallow up the older one as evidenced by these products announcements (which are real; we did not make them up): "They are so unique, we only made a few of them" and "It's so unique, it's almost one of a kind."

Unique is a unique word. We have no other adjective that easily and concisely conveys the sense of "one of a kind, unequaled." Because we already possess modifiers such as *unusual* and *distinctive*, there is no reason why *unique* should be wordnapped into their territory. If something is indeed quite unusual and almost one of a kind, write "quite unusual."

Sure, we who care know that we may be waging a losing battle, that *unique* may have already fallen before the onslaught of unusual. But we bewail the devaluing and potential loss of a wonderful word. If and when *unique* is completely emptied of its uniqueness, that change will have been tested against the disapproval of people like you and us, and the language will be the better for the give and take.

TEST YOURSELF

Circle the italicized word that works better (not best) on each sentence:

1. The weather should not *affect/effect* our plans, as billiards is played indoors.

2. Her estate will be divided *among/between* her five surviving cousins.

3. The list was *composed/comprised* of property owners only.

4. Is this quiz different *from/than* any other that you have ever taken?

5. For much of her childhood, the current world heptathlon champion was *disinterested/uninterested* in sports of any kind.

6. A bit *farther/further* down the road you will come to the Cracker Barrel Store.

7. I wish that there were *fewer/less* programs on television; they annoyingly interrupt the commercials.

8. From the tapes the jury *implied/inferred* that the broker was guilty.

9. For years, the huge unabridged dictionary has *laid/ lain* unused on his desk.

10. Lard-Away Elixir offers a *very unique/very unusual* opportunity to shed weight with absolutely no exercise or change in diet whatsoever.

--- **ANSWERS** ---

1. affect **2.** among **3.** composed **4.** from **5.** uninterested **6.** farther **7.** fewer **8.** inferred **9.** lain **10.** very unusual

□ 10 □

Sound-Alikes and Look-Alikes

What do you call a naked grizzly? A bare bear. What do you call a raspy-throated equine? A hoarse horse.

Homophones are words that sound the same but have different spellings and meanings. Considering the great number of sound-alikes and look-alikes in our word-rich English language, it is remarkable how many foreigners learn to speak and write English with such skill. Even native users can find themselves entangled in a briar patch of coincidences in sound and spelling.

A friend of ours once stopped to buy some writing supplies in Kansas and noticed that the gold-lettered sign on the window read "Stationary Store." She pointed out to the woman behind the counter, "*Stationery* refers to materials for writing, but *stationary* means 'immobile, unmoving, in one place.'"

"Well, honey," the clerk said as she returned the change, "we've been at this location for seventeen years." (But please note that, thanks to our friend's advice, the store owner did change the sign.)

A student once wrote in an essay, "They gave William IV a lovely funeral. It took six men to carry the beer." A single letter makes a world of difference between *bier* and

140

beer, changing the occasion from a sober to a rather merry one.

Homophones have always been mischievous, but with the advent of computer spelling checkers, they have become even sneakier. For example: *Hears a rye peace wee maid up in hour idyll thyme. Whee rote it four ewe too sea Howe homophones Cannes seam sew whiled, from there hare rite two they're tows. With pried wee no it will knot boar yew. Its meant too bee red allowed.*

Except for the proper names, our spell checkers didn't flag a single word in those italicized sentences. As writers, we are the ones who are left to make the necessary distinctions.

Look-alike words can be as vexatious as sound-alikes. Watch out or your *marital* life will become your *martial* life. You may wish to make a *simple* point, but you will seldom want to describe your arguments as *simplistic*. It may be true that, as a student wrote, "The automobile has had a beneficiary effect on the American family," but presumably that young scholar meant *beneficial*.

Here is a list of the most pesky sound-alikes and look-alikes, with the most confirmed troublemakers set in **bold-face** for easy identification. You'll note a number of words that we didn't have space to cover in the previous two chapters of this book. Consult your (up-to-date and reliable) dictionary about their meanings:

—— **A** ——

accept	**adverse**	**all together**
except	**averse**	**altogether**
adapt	**affect**	**allusion**
adopt	**effect**	**illusion**
advice	all ready	altar
advise	already	alter

amend	**appraise**	**assure**
emend	**apprise**	**ensure**
		insure
angel	ascent	
angle	assent	aural
		oral

————— B —————

bale	beach	**bloc**
bail	beech	**block**
baited	beat	boar
bated	beet	boor
		bore
bare	beer	
bear	bier	**born**
		borne
base	**berth**	
bass	**birth**	**breadth**
		breath
bazaar	bight	**breathe**
bizarre	bite	
	byte	bridal
		bridle

————— C —————

cache	**capital**	cede
cash	**capitol**	seed
callous	carat	ceiling
callus	caret	sealing
	carrot	
canvas	karat	cell
canvass		sell

censor	**chord**	**compose**
censure	**cord**	**comprise**
sensor	**cored**	
		conscience
cent	**cite**	**conscientious**
scent	**sight**	**conscious**
sent	**site**	
		consul
cereal	climactic	**council**
serial	climatic	**counsel**
chased	coarse	corps
chaste	course	corpse
childish	**complement**	cue
childlike	**compliment**	queue

—— **D** ——

dairy	deprecate	**discreet**
diary	depreciate	**discrete**
dam	**desert**	**disinterested**
damn	**dessert**	**uninterested**
dear	dew	dual
deer	do	duel
	due	
decent		
descent	**die**	
dissent	**dye**	
defuse	**disburse**	
diffuse	**disperse**	

— E —

elicit	**exalt**
illicit	**exult**
eminent	exercise
immanent	exorcize
imminent	

— F —

faint	**flaunt**	**foreword**
feint	**flout**	**forward**
fare	flea	**formally**
fair	flee	**formerly**
	flew	
farther		**fort**
further	flu	**forte**
	flue	
faze		fortunate
phase	**flounder**	fortuitous
	founder	
feat		**foul**
feet	flour	**fowl**
	flower	
fiscal		frees
physical	**forego**	freeze
	forgo	frieze
flair		
flare		

— G —

gaff	gait	gamble
gaffe	gate	gambol

gamut	gibe	grisly
gantlet	jibe	gristly
gauntlet	jive	grizzly
genes	gorilla	
jeans	guerrilla	
genteel	grill	
gentile	grille	
gentle		

—————— H ——————

hale	heard	holey
hail	herd	holly
		holy
hair	hew	wholly
hare	hue	
		home
hardy	hoard	hone
hearty	horde	
healthful	hoarse	
healthy	horse	
hear	hole	
here	whole	

—————— I ——————

idle	incite	instance
idol	insight	instants
idyll		
	ingenious	its
incidence	ingenuous	it's
incidents		

—— **J** ——

jam
jamb

—— **K** ——

key   knead   knot
quay   kneed   naught
               need   nought
knave   not
nave   knit
               nit

—— **L** ——

lacks   **lay**   load
lax   **lie**   lode

lam   leach   **loath**
lamb   leech   **loathe**

laps   **lead**   luxuriant
lapse   **led**   luxurious

later   lessen
latter   lesson

—— **M** ——

made   main   **manner**
maid   mane   **manor**

mail   maize   marquee
male   maze   marquis
                              marquise

masterful
masterly

might
mite

moot
mute

meat
meet
mete

militate
mitigate

moral
morale

miner
minor

muscle
mussel

medal
meddle
metal
mettle

missal
missile

—— N ——

naval
navel

nay
neigh

none
nun

—— O ——

oar
or
ore

official
officious

ordinance
ordnance

—— P ——

packed
pact

palate
pallet
palette

peak
peek
pique

pail
pale

passed
past

peal
peel

pane
pain

patience
patients

pedal
peddle
petal

pair
pare
pear

peace
piece

peer
pier

pidgin
pigeon

plain
plane

plum
plumb

poor
pore
pour

precede
proceed

prescribe
proscribe

preventative
preventive

principal
principle

profit
prophet

prostate
prostrate

––––– R –––––

rain
reign
rein

raise
rays
raze

rapped
rapt
wrapped

read
red

reek
wreak
wreck

rest
wrest

right
rite
write

ring
wring

role
roll

root
rout
route

rung
wrung

rye
wry

––––– S –––––

saver
savior
savor

scene
seen

serf
surf

sew
so
sow

sewage
sewerage

shear
sheer

shoe
shoo

shone
shown

slay
sleigh

soar
sore

spade
spayed

staff
staph

stake
steak

stationary
stationery

steal
steel

straight
strait

suit
suite
sweet

——— T ———

tale
tail

tare
tear

taught
taunt
taut

team
teem

tear
tier

than
then

their
there
they're

threw
through

thyme
time

to
too
two

toad
toed
towed

toe
tow

told
tolled

tortuous
torturous

turbid
turgid

troop
troupe

——— **V** ———

vain	vary	vice
vane	very	vise
vein		
	venal	viral
vale	venial	virile
veil		
	vial	
	vile	

——— **W** ———

wail	wander	wench
wale	wonder	winch
whale		
	ware	wet
waist	wear	whet
waste		
	way	which
wait	weigh	witch
weight		
	weather	whose
waive	wether	who's
wave	whether	

——— **Y** ———

yoke	yore
yolk	your
	you're

Test Yourself

Choose the correct word in each italicized pair:

1. The preacher made frequent *allusions/illusions* to the Bible.

2. I was *all together/altogether* delighted with my two-watt, blinking clown nose, *pedaled/peddled* to me by a professional clown.

3. The cat ate some pungent cheese, exhaled into the mousehole, and waited with *baited/bated* breath.

4. Pandora has the *bazaar/bizarre* theory that intelligence is determined by the size of one's ears.

5. At the *climactic/climatic* moment, the Roadrunner *fainted/feinted* left, then zoomed right, avoiding the clutches of the flabbergasted Coyote by a *hare's/hair's breadth/breath*.

6. If a cactus falls in the *desert/dessert*, does it make a sound?

7. The study of grammar can be divided into *discreet/discrete* and manageable entities.

8. Having a *flair/flare* for acting, Thorstein is never *fazed/phased* by speaking in front of large audiences.

9. Greta's *grisly/grizzly* jokes never fail to *elicit/illicit* shrieks of horror from her enthralled listeners.

10. The great movie palaces of the 1920s and 1930s were much more *luxuriant/luxurious than/then* the starkly functional multiplexes of today.

--- ANSWERS ---

1. allusions **2.** altogether, peddled **3.** baited *and* bated (both apply in this situation) **4.** bizarre **5.** climactic, feinted, hair's breadth **6.** desert **7.** discrete **8.** flair, fazed **9.** grisly, elicit **10.** luxurious, than

□ 11 □

The Strange Case of Pronouns

Pronouns are those all-purpose little words, such as *I*, *her*, and *yourself*, that spare us the trouble of having to write the name of a person, place, or thing again and again. As versatile as they are, however, pronouns present special problems to all who set pen to paper and fingers to keyboard. The reason lies both in the history of pronouns and in their ability—like the ability of Lon Chaney, Peter Sellers, Meryl Streep, Eddie Murphy, and Robin Williams—to appear in many guises and perform many roles, sometimes in the same sentence.

While the form of nouns has greatly simplified from Old English to Modern English, pronouns are more complicated. Today nouns remain the same in shape whether they be subjects or objects and change form only for possessives and plurals: *boy, boys, boy's, boys'*—four variations, two pronunciations. Pronouns, on the other hand, have retained more of their form changes. The first-person pronoun, for example, can exist as *I, me, my, mine, myself, we, us, our, ours, ourself,* and *ourselves*—eleven variations, eleven pronunciations.

To place the differences between nouns and pronouns in context, note that in the sentences "The man greeted the woman" and "The woman greeted the man" the changes in the functions of the nouns *man* and *woman* are indicated not by form but by word order. In the sentences "He greeted her" and "She greeted him," on the other hand, the third-person pronouns change form as they shift location and function.

This change of pronoun form to indicate function in a sentence (subject, object, possessive) is called pronoun case. Because pronouns assume so many more shapes than do nouns, these little words can trip up even the grammatically sure of foot.

Pronouns as Subjects

The personal pronouns *I, you, he, she, we,* and *they* are used as subjects. When talking about two persons, writers usually mention themselves second:

> She and *I* arranged every detail of the conference together.

> The Brownies and *we* had a disagreement about who would use the church basement that night.

When a personal pronoun is the subject of the omitted verb in an adverb clause of comparison, use the forms *I, he, she, we,* or *they*:

> Igor is even uglier than *I.*

> Fanga is more horrible than *she.*

Pronouns as Objects

The personal pronouns *me, you, him, her, us,* and *them* are used as objects:

> The committee invited Shaq and *me* to join the Olympic Dream Team.

> Between you and *me,* everyone except Garth and *her* enjoyed the Amazin' Amazon Mud Wrestle–Off.

Compound objects cause many a speaker and writer to use the wrong pronoun case:

> The committee invited Shaq and *I* to join the Olympic Dream Team.

> Between you and *I*, everyone except Garth and *she* enjoyed the Amazin' Amazon Mud Wrestle–Off.

To highlight the problem, remove a few words from each statement. No one would ever say, "The committee invited I" or "Between I" or "except she." Don't let compounds get on your case. Doubling the subject or object doesn't change the form of your pronouns.

The *Myself* Reflex

Ever wonder why so many speakers and writers misuse, abuse, and overuse the pronoun *myself*?: "They awarded the Good Citizen plaque to Melvin and myself"; "Priscilla and myself adore jelly beans." Red Smith, the graceful *New York Times* sportswriter, identified the reason most succinctly: "*Myself* is the foxhole of ignorance where cowards take refuge because they were taught that *me* is vulgar and *I* is egotistical."

The only three contexts in which *myself* should ever appear are:

(1) as a reflexive pronoun used as an object of a verb whose subject is the same: "She hurt *herself* climbing the walls of her home."

(2) as an intensifier: "I *myself* wouldn't be caught dead bungee jumping."

(3) in special idioms: "I slew the dragon all by *myself*."

Pronouns as Appositives

When a pronoun stands in apposition with (repeats) a subject, use *I*, *he*, *she*, *we*, or *they*. When a pronoun stands in apposition with an object, use *me*, *him*, *her*, *us*, or *them*:

> The whole family—Mom, Dad, Rosalie, and *I*—made plans to attend the Amazin' Amazon Mud Wrestle–Off.

> Uncle Sidney invited the whole family—Mom, Dad, Rosalie, and *me*—to attend the Amazin' Amazon Mud Wrestle–Off.

> *We* writers love nothing better than to craft a shining sentence.

> Nothing pleases *us* writers more than crafting a shining sentence.

Pronouns as Possessives

Which dog has the upper paw?:

a. A clever dog knows its master.
b. A clever dog knows it's master.

The answer is the dog in the second sentence, which states, "A clever dog knows that it is master."
Which is the greater compliment?:

a. I know your superior.
b. I know you're superior.

The answer is the second sentence, which states, "I know that you are superior."
Just as *yours*, *ours*, and *hers* are not apostrophized, *its* as a possessive pronoun has no apostrophe. *It's*, on the other hand, is a contraction of "it is" or "it has":

> A cat has claws at the end of *its* paws, while a comma is a pause at the end of *its* clause.

> "*It's* a beautiful day in the neighborhood," sang Mr. Rogers.

The most common goof occurs when *it's* is employed as a possessive pronoun. A full-page advertisement in *The New York Times* praised "the seasonless silks of Oscar de la Renta: parlor dressing at it's most pampered."

It is the same with *whose* and *who's*. *Whose* is the possessive form of *who*, while *who's* is a contraction of "who is" or "who has":

Are you the one *whose* dog chewed up the manuscript of my 1,500-page novel?

Knock knock. *Who's* there? Orange. Orange who? Orange you pleased to be reviewing the rules of English usage?

Pronouns with Gerunds

A gerund is an *-ing* form of a verb used as a noun, as in "I would never dream of cheating in solitaire." The possessive forms of the personal pronouns—*my, your, his, her, its, our,* and *their*—are used before gerunds when the gerund is the true object of the verb or preposition:

My friends were all surprised by *my* attending the Amazin' Amazon Mud Wrestle–Off.

Do you object to *their* attending the Amazin' Amazon Mud Wrestle–Off?

But:

I expected to find *him* cheering at the Amazin' Amazon Mud Wrestle–Off, but he wasn't anywhere in sight.

TEST YOURSELF

Choose the correct form of the pronoun in each sentence below:

1. Ophelia and *she/her* went to see *Rocky XII*.

2. The company sent *he/him/himself* and *I/me/myself* to the seminar.

3. It was *he/him/himself who/whom* I saw hiding behind the lamppost.

4. Between you and *I/me*, the form of a pronoun is important.

5. They had looked forward to *me/my* coming and were disappointed when I postponed my visit.

6. I saw *him/his* cheering at the Amazin' Amazon Mud Wrestle–Off.

7. Uncle Horace put up the whole family—my parents, Florence, and *I/me/myself*—for the weekend.

8. Should we—Grace, Brad, and *I/me/myself*—meet you at McDonald's after the seminar?

9. One of the most important benefits of college is the opportunity to talk to those who know more than *I/me/myself*.

10. The lawyer told *we/us* boys to say nothing about the accident.

——————————————— ANSWERS ———————————————

1. *She* is part of the compound subject of the verb *went*.

2. *Him* and *me* form the compound direct object of the verb *sent*.

3. *It* is an expletive, a dummy subject, and *he* is the real subject of the main clause. In formal writing, purists still consider "it was he" superior to "it was him." *Whom* is the object of *I saw*. (We'll cover *who* and *whom* in the next chapter.)

4. *Me* is the object of the preposition *between*.

5. As the object of the preposition *to, coming* is a gerund, an *-ing* form of a verb that functions as a noun. Pronouns preceding gerunds assume the possessive form, in this case *my.*

6. Here *him* is the object of the verb *saw*, and *cheering* is not a gerund but a participle.

7. The appositives stand in apposition with *family* and should agree in case. Because *family* is a direct object of the verb *put up*, the pronoun form should be *me*.

8. Here the appositives should agree with the subject *we*. Hence, *I.*

9. *I* kicks off an adverbial clause of comparison and is the subject of the understood verb *do*.

10. Because *boys* is the direct object of the verb *told*, the pronoun appositive should be cast as *us*.

References Wanted

The following examples are real. They actually appeared in print. We did not make them up. Notice how the italicized pronouns are used in these sentences:

> After Governor Baldwin watched the lion perform, *he* was taken to Main Street and fed 25 pounds of raw meat in front of the Cross Keys Theater.

> On the floor above *him* lived a redheaded instructor in physical education, whose muscular calves he admired when *they* nodded to each other by the mailbox.

In the first sentence, who was taken to Main Street—the lion or the governor? In the second sentence, who nodded to each other—the man and the redheaded instructor or her muscular calves?

Every pronoun must have a clear antecedent, a noun or pronoun to which to refer. If the reference is not clear, the result is likely to be comic or puzzling. The comedy or confusion that results from ambiguous pronoun references can be cleared up by replacing the ambiguous pronoun with a noun:

> After Governor Baldwin watched the lion perform, the animal was taken to Main Street and fed 25 pounds of raw meat in front of the Cross Keys Theater.

or by recasting the sentence:

> On the floor above him lived a redheaded instructor in physical education. When they nodded to each other by the mailbox, he admired her muscular calves.

TEST YOURSELF

The following sentences are also authentic disasters. Repair each statement by eliminating ambiguous or vague reference of pronouns:

1. Recent visitors were the Jonathan Goldings and their in-laws, the Brett Packards, from Lake Placid, New York. Brett had his tonsils removed in Centerville. It was pleasant to have them for supper.

2. The duchess handled the launching beautifully, confidently smashing the champagne against the prow. The crowd cheered as she majestically slid down the greasy runway into the sea.

3. Antinuclear protestors released live cockroaches inside the White House Friday, and they were arrested when they left and blocked a security gate.

4. We have turned cans into cash to use toward programs for our children, rather than burying them in a landfill.

5. We do not tear your clothing with machinery: we do it carefully by hand.

ANSWERS
---

1. Recent visitors were the Jonathan Goldings and their in-laws, the Brett Packards, from Lake Placid, New York. Brett had his tonsils removed in Centerville. It was pleasant to have **the Packards** for supper.

2. The duchess handled the launching beautifully, confidently smashing the champagne against the prow. The crowd cheered as **the ship** majestically slid down the greasy runway into the sea.

3. Antinuclear protestors released live cockroaches inside the White House Friday. **The protestors** were arrested when they left and blocked a security gate.

4. We have turned cans into cash to use toward programs for our children, rather than burying **the cans** in a landfill.

5. We do not tear your clothing with machinery; we **wash your items** carefully by hand.

The Great Pronoun Debates

Writers, particularly professional writers, are in a sense custodians of language. Just as a sensible person does not buy a new wardrobe with every fashion fad, a wise writer does not eagerly embrace every word and phrase fad and every departure from conventional usage. In both fashion and writing, prudent people will heed the advice of Alexander Pope:

> *Be not the first by whom the new are tried,*
> *Nor yet the last to lay the old aside.*

Of all the parts of speech, pronouns assume the greatest variety of forms. Thus, they present the greatest challenge to you as a writer. Here are six of the most controversial pronoun decisions:

Sex and the Single Pronoun

Attention, writers.

Anyone who wants to be labeled as sexist please raise *his* hand.

Anyone who wants to be labeled as tedious please raise *his or her* hand.

Anyone who wants to be labeled as ungrammatical please raise *their* hand.

Is there no other choice? Can't we write a simple sentence without being labeled "sexist," "tedious," or "ungrammatical"?

Anyone is a singular pronoun. Traditionally it has been followed by the masculine pronoun *he* when it applies to either male or female, as in the first of the sentences above. But in modern society a writer who adheres to this tradition is subject to being labeled as sexist. While many good writers still prefer the embracive *he*, you should be aware that an increasing number of readers find the pronoun offensive.

Language is the window through which we look out at the world. Language has the power to shape our world even as our world is shaping language. Among the personal pronouns—first-, second-, and third-person singular and plural—only one, the third-person singular, identifies the sex of the individual. Many studies indicate that *man* as the inclusive noun and *he* as the inclusive pronoun create images of males to the exclusion of females.

The *his-or-her* solution is a safe answer, but it is the first step on the road to gracelessness and tedium. Writers who stuff several pairings of *his or her, him or herself,* and the like into a sentence are not just flouting grace, they're flaunting the tedium of their prose.

We have little doubt that *anyone . . . their* is destined to become good, idiomatic English. It already pervades the speech of educated Americans, and daily it grows more common in writing. In his delightful little book *Fumblerules*, language guru William Safire derides that kind of construction on one page but uses it unselfconsciously on another: "Here's the best way to proofread copy: Get *somebody* else to do it. If necessary, do it with *them,* reading aloud to each other." (Emphasis added.) The grammatically conservative *New York Times* allowed the following sentence on its pages: "But *everyone* seemed too busy with *their* oral sneers and jousts to pay much attention to his pleas." (Emphasis added.)

The third edition of England's classic *Copy Editing: The Cambridge Handbook for Editors, Authors and Publishers* announces, "An example where *they* provides the simplest, clearest solution is: 'Each author presented an evening of readings from their work.'" Similarly, the *Columbia Guide to Standard American English* supports the sentence "Each person must bring their own calculator."

Once you set yourself to it, you will soon find it quite natural to use *humankind* in place of *mankind*, *letter carrier* in place of *mailman*, and *they* in place of *he* or *he or she*. Your mind will naturally slip into a mode that will allow you to recast your statements judiciously, even elegantly, and to avoid sexism:

> Please raise your hand if you want to be labeled . . .

> If you want to be labeled . . . please raise your hand.

> All who want to be labeled . . . please raise your hands.

> All writers who want to be labeled . . . please raise their hands.

> We writers who want to be labeled . . . should raise our hands.

"It Is I" versus "It Is Me": Do the *I*'s Have It?

A man appears at the Pearly Gates. Saint Peter calls out, "Who goes there?"

"It is I," announces the man.

"Oh, no," moans Saint Peter. "Not another one of those English teachers."

The rivalry between "It is I" and "It is me" has provoked a long-running debate among word mavens. Supporters of "It is I" contend that forms of the verb *to be*, such as *is* and *was*, should unfailingly be followed by pronouns cast in the nominative case, *I* in this instance. Those in the corner of "It is me" counter with the argument that pronoun cases have become so weakened that the force of word order now overrides the force of case. When a pronoun appears in the object part (end) of a sentence, more and more writers are using "It's me" and "It is us." Walt Kelly's immortal Pogo once proclaimed, "We have met the enemy and he is us!" Those who would prefer "We have met the enemy and he is we!" are the same tin-eared folks who wish Sammy Davis had sung, "I Gotta Be I."

For most people, though, "It's me" is habitual and needs no apology. After all, the French have always said, "*C'est moi*," not "*C'est je*." Know your audience well and choose your pronoun thoughtfully. If the *I*'s have it, use *I*, but don't force the issue in conversation or informal writing.

Who versus *That*: Getting Personal

Ordinarily, use the relative pronouns *who*, *whose*, and *whom* to refer to persons and animals and use *that* or *which* to refer to things. Some writers employ *that* for persons, but we are not among them. *That* seems too impersonal for persons:

> The clerk *who* had sold me two left shoes was booted from his job.

> The child *whom* we scolded blushed a fiery red.

> I didn't see the Frisbee *that* knocked off my hat.

> The aftershock, *which* came a day after the quake, registered 6.3 on the Richter scale.

Who versus *Whom*: For *Who* the Bell Tolls

In one installment of the *Nancy* comic strip, the frizzy-haired heroine is writing a letter that begins, "To who it may concern . . ." The worried Nancy then crosses out the *who* and changes it to *whome*, and then to *whoom*. With a frustrated "Grrr!" she finally settles on the salutation "Dear you all."

In a *Peanuts* episode we see an open-eyed Charlie Brown in bed thinking, "Sometimes I lie awake at night and ask, 'Is it all worth it?' . . . Then a voice says, 'Who are you talking to?' . . . Then another voice says, 'You mean, "To who are you talking?"' . . . No wonder I lie awake at night!"

More than fifty years ago, Professor Arthur H. Weston composed this ditty:

> *It's hard to devise an appropriate doom*
> *For those who say* who *when they ought to say* whom.
> *But it's even more hard to decide what to do*
> *With those who say* whom *when they ought to say* who.

Times have changed. Author Calvin Trillin claims that "*whom* is a word that was invented to make everyone sound like a butler. Nobody who is not a butler has ever said it out loud without feeling just a little bit weird."

William Safire has announced the doom of *whom*. Quoth the maven: "Look: I've never pretended to have a handle on *who-whom*. . . . Let us resolve to follow Safire's Rule on Who-Whom: whenever *whom* sounds correct, recast the sentence."

When we are asked for who the bell tolls, we are reluctant to answer, "It tolls for *whom*." *Whom* may one day disappear entirely—but not yet, at least not yet in formal writing. When the pronoun is used as a subject or predicate nominative (linked to a subject by a verb such as *is*), the form should be *who*. When the pronoun is used as an object—direct, indirect, or of a preposition—the word in formal writing is *whom*. Seems so simple, but it isn't.

Thinking that *whom* is a sign of superior grammar and breeding, a semiliterate snob in *A Thurber Carnival* asks, "Whom do you think you are, anyways?" Demonstrating its skittishness about the *who/whom* confusion, a Connecticut newspaper hedges its bets with this sentence: "Mr. Beeston said he was asked to step down, although it was not known exactly who or whom asked him." We'll bet on *who*, the subject of the verb *asked* in the noun clause "who asked him."

All this industrial-strength grammar notwithstanding, you can usually ignore *whom* in speech without raising too many eyebrows, except where a preposition immediately precedes the pronoun. But for some readers you will want to learn to use *who* and *whom* correctly in writing. It's really not too difficult. Maybe one day the old pronoun *whom* will fade away. Until then, why not show this venerable word some respect?

Test Yourself

Do you say *who* when you ought to say *whom*, and *whom* when you ought to say *who*? Find out by choosing the correct pronoun form in each of the sentences below:

1. *Who/Whom* do you think was killed in more movies—Jason or Freddy Krueger?

2. We don't know *who/whom* to trust.

3. There goes the lineman *who/whom* the coach believes is the team's most valuable player.

4. I'll pledge my support to *whoever/whomever* promises to protect the environment.

5. We all wondered about *who/whom* the intruders were.

ANSWERS

1. *Who* is the subject of the passive verb "was killed." The clause "do you think" has no effect on the grammar of the main clause.

2. *Whom* is the object of the infinitive *to trust*.

3. *Who* is the subject of the verb *is*. Again, the clause "the coach believes" has no effect on the grammar of the main clause.

4. The entire noun clause, "*whoever* promises to protect the environment," is the object of the preposition *to*, but every clause must have a subject, and *whoever* is the subject of the verb *promises*.

5. The noun clause "*who* the intruders were" is the object of the preposition *about*. Within the noun clause *who* functions as a predicate nominative.

That versus *Which*: Beware the Wicked *Which*

Not every writer makes a distinction between *that* and *which* as relative pronouns used to introduce adjective clauses, but there is a difference and it is worth preserving.

Clauses that identify and limit (that is, define) the words they modify are called restrictive and are not introduced by a comma: "This is the manuscript *that I told you about*." Clauses that merely add explanatory information and do not identify the words they modify are called nonrestrictive and are preceded by a comma: "This is John's newest story, *which I'm using in the next issue*." For many centuries, *that* and *which* as relative pronouns were used interchangeably to introduce restrictive and nonrestrictive clauses. Nowadays, they are still used indiscriminately to lead off restrictive clauses—"This is the manuscript *that* I told you about"; "This is the manuscript *which* I told you about"— while *which* is greatly preferred to introduce nonrestrictive clauses—"This is John's newest story, *which* [not *that*] I'm using in the next issue."

Having presented a review of the history of these two relative pronouns, we recommend that you use *that* to introduce restrictive adjective clauses and *which* to introduce nonrestrictive clauses. To our eyes and ears (and, we hope, to yours) *that* looks and sounds more defining and more assertive than *which*. *That* more powerfully bonds an adjective clause to its antecedent and is, in general, the more appropriate lead for restrictive clauses. *That*, on the other hand, is too emphatic to introduce nonrestrictive, merely descriptive clauses. This sentence is one *that* illustrates the difference, *which* can have an effect on the sound of your writing.

We place commas before and after a nonrestrictive clause because the voice would ordinarily pause at that point: "This is the house that Jack built" (no pause before the adjective clause: hence no commas); but "Jack's house, which sits on a hillside, is exquisite" (pause before the clause; hence commas). When we see a sentence such as "this is the manuscript which I told you about," we hear a distracting lull before the *which*. *Which* strikes us as simply too tentative to kick off a restrictive statement.

Restatement of rule: If the clause is to be set off by commas (nonrestrictive) and refers to things, use *which*. Otherwise, use *that*.

TEST YOURSELF

Provide *which*, *that*, or *who* for each blank and properly punctuate each sentence:

1. It is the principle of identifying the antecedent _____ distinguishes restrictive from nonrestrictive clauses.

2. In the days before the Civil War, many Northerners _____ wanted war were not enthusiastic abolitionists.

3. Democratic elections _____ are central to our system of government are not always easy to ensure in a nation _____ is just beginning to experiment with government of the people, by the people, and for the people.

4. Men _____ are notoriously inept as cooks should be kept out of the kitchen.

5. The sport _____ is most rapidly capturing the public's fancy is golf, _____ now boasts more participants than tennis.

—————————— ANSWERS ——————————

1. It is the principle of identifying the antecedent **that** distinguishes restrictive from nonrestrictive clauses. (restrictive clause)

2. In the days before the Civil War, many Northerners **who** wanted war were not enthusiastic abolitionists. (restrictive clause)

3. Democratic elections, **which** are central to our system of government, are not always easy to ensure in a nation **that** is just beginning to experiment with government of the people, by the people, and for the people. (nonrestrictive clause, restrictive clause)

4. Men **who** are notoriously inept as cooks should be kept out of the kitchen. (restrictive clause) Or if you feel that all men are inept cooks and, hence, that the adjective clause is nonrestrictive: Men, **who** are notoriously inept as cooks, should be kept out of the kitchen.

5. The sport **that** is most rapidly capturing the public's fancy is golf, **which** now boasts more participants than tennis. (restrictive clause, nonrestrictive clause)

"None Is" versus "None Are:" The *None* Story

Lightning never strikes twice in the same place. Handling a frog gives you warts. *None* is always singular. No one knows who set these superstitions loose, but loose they are.

The cause of the last piece of hoodoo, voodoo, and doodoo is the belief that *none* is simply a contraction of "no one" or "not one" and, hence, must take a singular verb. Context disproves this theory, however.

Examine these sentences: "None of the work was completed." "None of his theory makes any sense." In these statements, *none* doesn't mean "not one," but rather "not any" or "no part of."

But what about sentences in which *none* refers to groups

of people or things? In these instances, virtually every authority—the Oxford, Merriam-Webster's, and American Heritage dictionaries and Fowler and Bernstein—agrees that *none* can be followed by a singular or a plural verb, according to its setting. In fact, many guidebooks maintain that the plural is more often called for than the singular.

When you wish to emphasize that *none* means "not a single one," use a singular verb: "We sampled many brands of ice cream, but none was as delicious as High-Cal." When you use *none* to mean "several" or "a group of" or "not any," employ a plural verb, as Andrew Marvell did when he wrote: "The grave's a fine and private place, / But none, I think, do there embrace."

□ 13 □

Improve Your Verb-al Skills

A verb is a word or group of words that makes a statement or asks a question or issues a command. Because every complete sentence must have a verb, either expressed or implied, you can't write home without them.

As the words in a sentence that express existence, action, or movement, verbs are the spark plugs of effective style. If you want those spark plugs to fire effectively, you'll want to be sure that no ungrammatical muck clogs their firing.

Seeking Full Agreement

Which statement is correct?:

a. Nine and seven is fifteen.
b. Nine and seven are fifteen.

The answer (gotcha!?) is that both statements are correct grammatically, and neither is correct mathematically. Nine and seven is—or are—*sixteen*.

Studies indicate that mistakes in subject-verb agreement are among the commonest errors in writing.

A subject that means one person or thing takes a singular verb:

Only one vampire bat *remains* in the cave.

The Bible *is* the best-selling book of all time.

Compound subjects joined by *and* usually take a plural verb:

Here *come* the lions and tigers and bears.

Are Caligula and Nero still your favorite emperors?

But when the parts of a compound subject are thought of as almost inseparable, use a singular verb:

Bacon and eggs *is* my—but not my digestive system's—favorite breakfast.

Fresh air and sunshine *was* what she needed.

When the parts of a compound subject joined by *or* or *nor* are singular, the subject is considered singular:

Is Caligula or Nero your favorite emperor?

Neither Caligula nor Nero *is* my favorite emperor.

When the parts of a compound subject joined by *or* or *nor* are plural, or the one nearer is plural, use a plural verb:

Hotdogs and hamburgers *are* less bother to prepare.

Neither the dictionary nor the reference books *were* of any help.

But:

Neither the reference books nor the dictionary *was* of any help.

A singular subject takes a singular verb even when a phrase beginning with *together with, in addition to, as well as*, and the like comes between the subject and the verb:

The CEO, as well as every member of the board of directors, *was* present at the annual meeting.

In careful writing, the construction "one of those who" takes a plural verb that agrees in number with the antecedent of *who*:

I am one of those wannabe athletes who *fail* in every sport.

Here the formal logic is that if you transpose the sentence, you come out with "Of those wannabe athletes who *fail* in every sport, I am one."

The verb *to be* agrees in number with the subject, not with the noun or pronoun that comes after:

A complete game *is* four quarters of fifteen minutes each.

Twelve weekly lectures *are* a heavy teaching load.

Collective Anxiety

Editor Horace Greeley demanded that his reporters on the *New York Tribune* treat *news* as a plural noun. "Are there any news?" Greeley once cabled a field reporter.

The reporter fired back this message: "No, not a single new."

The news *is* that some writers are troubled by collectives, nouns that are singular in form but may take either a singular or plural verb. Among the most familiar examples of such groups, persons, and things are *band*, *choir*, *committee*, *couple*, *crowd*, *faculty*, *family*, *group*, *jury*, *majority*, and *total*.

Whether to use a singular or plural verb form with a collective depends on what the writer has in mind: To show that the individuals are a group, use a plural verb; to show a group as a single unit, use a singular verb. In "The couple were married in 1987," *were* is preferred because we think of two individuals joined in marriage. In "While jogging through the park, the couple was attacked," we think of the couple as a unit.

With a collective noun such as *committee*, as in "The

committee is/are well qualified to select art for the new office," choose either the singular or plural form, depending on whether you're thinking of the qualifications of the individual members or the qualifications of the committee as a whole. The best way to determine which verb is appropriate is to ask yourself what you want to say to the reader. In many instances, the difference won't be worth worrying about.

Names of diseases that end in s, such as *measles*, *mumps*, and *rickets*, are always singular. More *ic*ky are nouns ending in *ics*, such as *acoustics*, *athletics*, *economics*, *graphics*, *linguistics*, *mathematics*, *physics*, and *statistics*. When these terms refer to a field of study or body of knowledge, they take a singular verb:

> Acoustics *is* a science to which architects pay heed when they design theater halls.

> Politics *is* a slippery but fascinating subject.

But:

> The acoustics in the Mormon Tabernacle *are* famous.

> The office politics in this company *detract* from the pursuit of excellence.

With group nouns such as *number*, the controlling words are *the* and *a(n)*. Choose the singular verb with *the*, the plural verb with *a(n)*:

> The greatest number of complaints about tax increases *come* from the middle class.

> A great number of complaints about tax increases *comes* from the middle class.

Singular or Plural?

The adjectives *each*, *every*, *either*, and *neither* and the indefinite pronouns *anybody*, *anyone*, *each*, *everyone*, *nobody*, *no one, somebody,* and *someone* are singular and generally take singular verbs and pronouns:

Every bear and woodchuck *sleeps* through the winter.

Neither of the cars *seems* worth the price.

I wonder if anyone *is* home; everyone *seems* to be gone.

When plural nouns denoting time periods *(hours, months, years),* amount *(bushels, gallons, tons),* measure *(feet, yards, miles),* and weight *(ounces, pounds, tons)* are thought of a single unit, they take a singular verb:

Two days *seems* like forever to a two-year-old.

Four yards *was* not enough cloth for the dress.

A few common words taken directly from Greek and Latin have plurals that are not always recognized as plurals. *Criteria, phenomena,* and *alumni* are the plurals for *criterion, phenomenon,* and *alumnus.* Use "The criteria (or phenomena or alumni) is . . ." and risk the opprobrium of those who know better. *Data* and *bacteria* are plural, but because their singular forms—*datum* and *bacterium*—are rarely seen except in academic and scientific writing, *data* and *bacteria* are more often than not used with a singular verb form. Using *data* and *bacteria* with a plural verb form, as in "The data for the O. J. Simpson case are not all in" and "The bacteria are spreading rapidly," seems pretentious to some people even though it is still common. We, your reader-friendly authors, have a bias toward preserving the classical heritage in our language. Still, we'll say here what we have said throughout the book: Know your audience and use the more appropriate form.

TEST YOURSELF

In each sentence, choose the singular or plural verb:

1. Bread and butter *taste/tastes* better with jam on top.

2. Neither the Snaggle twins nor Tabatha *was/were* informed of the changes made in the club bylaws.

3. Three hours *is/are* a long time to wait in line.

4. There *go/goes* the elephants.

5. She is one of those women who *insists/insist* on shattering the glass ceiling installed by her corporation.

6. The criteria for excellent writing *has/have* much in common with the criteria for effective speaking.

7. Having coffee and doughnuts in the office each morning *is/are* something we all look forward to.

8. Her purse, along with her checkbook and all her credit cards, *was/were* stolen.

9. Physics *is/are* among the most difficult subjects I have studied.

10. Neither of the experiments *appears/appear* to confirm the feasibility of cold fusion.

──────────────── ANSWERS ────────────────

1. *Tastes.* Here the parts of the compound subject constitute one thing.

2. *Was.* Of the two subjects joined by *nor*, *Tabatha*, the nearer to the verb, is singular.

3. *Is.* Here *three hours* is a single unit.

4. *Go.* Even with the transposition of subject and verb, the plural subject requires a plural verb. Pay heed to this rule especially in constructions beginning with *there* and *here*.

5. *Insist.* In general, the adjective clause modifies the closer antecedent, here *women*.

6. *Have.* The verb must agree with the plural noun, *criteria*.

7. *Is.* Despite the intervention of "coffee and doughnuts," *having* is a gerund requiring a singular verb.

8. *Was.* The information set off by the commas modifies the subject, *purse*, but does not change its singularity.

9. *Is. Physics* is a singular subject.

10. *Appears.* Here the adjective *neither* requires a singular verb.

Tense Times with Verbs

The fourth most popular film of the summer of 1989 was *Honey, I Shrunk the Kids*, a title that threatens to erase centuries of development of those strong, irregular verbs whose internal vowels inflect so mellifluously. A national sports report began, "The Chicago Bulls did the major bartering and the Washington Bullets shedded half their front court." When interviewed right after booting a long field goal that won the 1991 National Football Conference championship, New York Giants kicker Matt Bahr said, "It really hasn't sank—or is it sunk?—in yet."

Shrunk, *bored*, *shedded*, and *sank* are but four examples of the verbal potholes into which even professional writers stumble when they form the past tenses of certain verbs. Let's take a historical (not "an historical") look at the problem:

English verbs are traditionally divided into two great classes, according to the ways they form their past tense and past participle. Strong, irregular verbs are so called because they have within them the capacity to change tense without recourse to an ending. Such verbs usually travel into the past by way of a change in a vowel and form their past participles by another vowel shift and, in many cases, adding *-n* or *-en*: *begin-began-begun*; *write-wrote-written*. Weak, regular verbs exhibit a pattern in which the vowel doesn't change, but *-d*, *-ed*, or *-t* is affixed to form the past tense and past participle: *walk-walked-walked*; *bend-bent-bent*.

To complicate the picture, some verbs undergo both a change in vowel sound and an adding of *-d* or *-t*: *lose-lost-*

lost; teach-taught-taught. Others don't change at all: *set-set-set; put-put-put*.

Over time, we have come to accept the weak, regular verb sequence as the normal pattern so that all new verbs that enter the English language are invariably conjugated by simply adding *-ed* or *-d*, as in *radio-radioed* and *televise-televised*. The weak, regular pattern has become the norm while many strong, irregular verbs of the *shrink-shrank-shrunk* pattern remain prominent in our language to confound and confuse us.

Rather than feeling tense about tenses, use your ears—and a good dictionary.

Test YOURSELF

Now it's time for an in-tense quiz. Here are twelve troublemaking verbs that become nettlesome as they go back in time. Identify the past-tense form (or forms) of each verb:

1.	dive	**7.**	sneak
2.	fly	**8.**	spring
3.	hang	**9.**	swim
4.	kneel	**10.**	tread
5.	light	**11.**	wake
6.	shine	**12.**	weave

ANSWERS

1. Either the regular *dived* or the irregular *dove* is acceptable.

2. *Flew*, unless you're speaking or writing about a baseball game. Then it's *flied*, as in "The batter flied out to left field."

3. *Hung* or *hanged*. Many a purist would insist that pictures are hung and cattle rustlers were hanged. Judges did sentence with this sentence: "You shall be hanged by the neck until dead."

4. *Knelt* or *kneeled*. Many verbs in English change a long *e* sound in the present-tense form to a short *e* and add a *t* or *d* sound to form the past tense: *sleep-slept, flee-fled*. In almost all such verbs, the short *e* past-tense form is required. There are, however, three common verbs that may form the past tense by adding *-ed* or by shortening the *e* and adding *t*: *kneeled* or *knelt, dreamed* or *dreamt*, and *leaped* or *leapt*.

5. *Lighted* or *lit*. Ernest Hemingway's "A Clean, Well-Lit Place" would have been just as bright.

6. Again meaning determines form. If the verb is intransitive and means "to radiate," the past-tense form is *shone*, as in "The sun shone all day long." If the verb is transitive and means "to polish," the form is *shined*, as in "In the army, I shined my shoes every day."

7. *Sneaked* or *snuck*, although some purists and dictionaries label *snuck* as "colloquial" or "substandard." It isn't.

8. *Sprang* may be a trifle more appropriate a past tense for violent action—"The dog sprang at the intruder"—and *sprung* for simple growing —"Overnight a thorn bush sprung up."

9. As is the case with *shrink-shrank-shrunk, swam* is preferable to *swum* in the past tense, with *swum* reserved for the past participle.

10. *Trod* or *treaded*, but the form for swimming is always "She treaded water."

11. *Wake* and its close kin *awake* are two verbs still in ferment. The past-tense *woke* and *awoke* are now more usual than *waked* and *awaked*—"I woke up to the sound of a roaring train." In American English, *woken* and *awoken* and, less commonly, *wakened* and *awakened* are all used for the past participle.

12. Generally *wove* and *weaved* are interchangeable. Many speakers and writers tend to use "He wove a rug" and, when the literal act of weaving is immaterial, "Her car weaved its way through traffic."

Should Nouns Be Verbed?

Many well-meaning people concerned about the state of the English language react with horror against any noun that has turned into a verb. But part of the genius of English is words that can rail-jump from one part of speech to another with no apparent change in form. We say, "Let's wallpaper the room this morning" instead of the more cumbersome "Let's put wallpaper on the walls of the room this morning."

Folks used to get huffy and puffy about the verbs *to contact* and *to process*, but today who minds? What exactly is wrong with "Tom Hanks will host *Saturday Night Live* this week"? Is "Tom Hanks will be the host of *Saturday Night Live* this week" demonstrably superior?

We simply ask that you avoid blanket judgments and evaluate each noun-into-verb shift one case at a time. The converted verbs *to parent*, *to party*, and *to total* (an automobile), for example, appear to be wonderful additions to the language. On the other hand, does *to finalize* add anything to the language that *to complete* or *to finish* hasn't already supplied? What does *to author* accomplish that *to write* doesn't?

These days all we hear about is that something *impacts* something else. What has happened to that sturdy standby *to affect*? We stand by popular linguist Charles Harrington Elster, who laments, "Once upon a time we expressed the influence of something calmly and clearly by saying that it had an effect, or that it affected something else. Now it is hammered into our heads day in and day out with the word *impact*. Are we wholly deaf to the subtlety of language? Why do we insist on using a pile driver when a putty knife will do?"

The Moody Subjunctive

English verbs assume three moods—indicative, imperative, and subjunctive. A verb in the indicative mood shows that the sentence is regarded as a statement or question about an actual thing or occurrence: "I love you." Commands assume verbs in the imperative mood: "Love me." Finally, we cast verbs in the subjunctive mood in statements that are regarded as contrary to fact or highly unlikely: "I wish that Tom Cruise were in love with me."

While Latin, French, German, and Old English possess elaborate subjunctive scaffolding, the subjunctive mood has become stripped down and rather rickety in contemporary English. Some grammarians, in fact, consider the subjunctive as obsolete as spats and mustache cups, but it is often preserved in educated speech and writing and preferred by educated listeners and readers.

Employ the subjunctive:

- in noun clauses that begin with *that* and follow verbs such as *demand*, *recommend*, *require*, and *wish*: "I demand that he *resign* immediately"; "I wish I *were* home."
- in some idiomatic expressions: "*Be* that as it may . . ."
- to express conditions contrary to fact or highly unlikely, especially in *if* and *though* adverbial clauses: "If only I *were* president . . ." ; "She acted as though she *were* president."

In most instances, your ear will tell you when a subjunctive verb is required, but the most common misuse of the subjunctive—and one more likely to be perpetrated by an educated person—results from the misconception that an *if*-clause is always followed by the subjunctive verb *were*.

"If I *were* you" is a clearly impossible condition and requires a subjunctive verb. "If the United States *were* a monarchy, the White House would be the White Castle and George Washington's descendants would be occupying the throne." Again the subjunctive form, *were*, is the proper choice because the United States is not a monarchy. But when the sentence states a real condition, rather than a hypothetical one, the indicative is called for:

"Wherever she went, he followed her. If she *was* walking in the park, he was there, sprawled on a bench. If she *was* shopping in the supermarket, he was there, staring from the produce section." The indicative form, *was*, is the correct choice because the statement is not contrary to fact: She actually *was* walking and shopping.

For more than a century, latter-day grammarians have been announcing the extinction of the subjunctive mood, but, like *whom*, it lives, probably because educated people keep it alive, even if they do misuse it sometimes. We advise that you use it according to the conventions outlined above and disregard it when it seems to make your writing sound unnatural.

TEST YOURSELF

Now show that you can control the moody subjunctive. Choose the correct verb in each sentence that follows.

1. We ask that writers, who are paid so sporadically, *are/be* allowed to income-average.

2. We suggest that each writer *receive/receives* a bonus for each rejection letter.

3. Our fifteen-year-old wishes he *was/were* old enough to drive.

4. If I *was/were* you, I wouldn't buy a house right now.

5. If it *was/were* raining at Wimbledon yesterday, the tennis matches were probably postponed.

——————————— ANSWERS ———————————

1. be **2.** receive **3.** were **4.** were **5.** was

Shall We Use *Shall*?

Excepting questions such as "What shall we do?" and "Shall we begin?," *shall* has all but disappeared from American English. In its traditional uses, *shall* sounds affected, almost prissy, to our ears. Because the reputed distinctions between *shall* and *will* are just too complicated to bother with, *will* and *would* have replaced *shall* and *should* in most cases. Writer Christopher Morley once quipped, "I own two cats named Shall and Will because nobody can tell them apart."

In legal documents *shall* is used to express mandate. "The seller shall deliver a clear title to the property at the time of closing" means, in effect, that the seller is required to deliver a clear title; "The seller will deliver a clear title" is a simple statement of what is expected to happen. Some writers, in a misguided effort to give their writing a legal flavor, will toss about a few *shall*s. It sounds—and is—phony and officious. Leave *shall* to the lawyers.

□ 14 □

Modify Your Words

"When you catch an adjective, kill it," wrote Mark Twain. "No, I don't mean utterly, but kill most of them—then the rest will be valuable."

Adjectives and adverbs do have their value for describing what goes on in our lives. In standard English, writers and speakers use adjectives to modify nouns and pronouns, and adverbs to modify verbs, adjectives, and other adverbs:

I was *sure* it was a good car; it *surely* runs well.

This is a *really* good car with *real* leather seats.

Sometimes words that look like adjectives function as adverbs naturally and idiomatically:

Go *slow*.

They play *rough* with their get-rich-*quick* schemes.

Use *first*, *second*, and *third*, rather than *firstly*, *secondly*, and *thirdly*. As an adverb, *more important*, a shortening of *What is more important*, is preferable to *more importantly*. But "She hit the baseball good and ran quick" will not cut it outside the sports broadcasting booth (and we're not ecstatic about such flattened adverbs *inside* that booth).

When you "put your best foot forward," you extend one of two feet, and "may the best team win" usually refers to one of two teams. Except for such ingrained idioms, use the comparative forms of adjectives and adverbs in writing of two persons or things:

hotter　more brilliant　earlier　more efficiently

Use superlative forms in writing about more than two persons or things:

hottest　most brilliant　earlier　most efficiently

Be aware that a few adjectives and adverbs have irregular forms:

good/well-better-best　bad-worse-worst
far-farther-farthest

Don't Dangle Your Participles in Public

Phrases and clauses can act as adjectives and adverbs:

Former hostage Terry Waite talked *with Barbara Walters about his five years of confinement in Beirut.*

Driving through Yellowstone Park, we saw many bears.

Unfortunately, the two sentences above appeared in a newspaper and a student essay as:

Former hostage Terry Waite talked about his five years of confinement in Beirut with Barbara Walters.

We saw many bears driving through Yellowstone Park.

Was Terry Waite confined with Barbara Walters in Beirut? Of course not. Rather, she interviewed him about the experience.

Who was driving through Yellowstone Park? We, not the bears.

Such grisly sentences are afflicted with misplaced modifiers, causing their scaffolding to be firmly planted on midair. We've said it before, and we're saying it here again: Tuck in your shirt and tuck your modifiers securely into each sentence.

Test Yourself

Each of the following sentences has appeared in newspaper articles or student compositions, and each contains a misplaced or dangling modifier. Relocate or undangle each modifier.

1. Abraham Lincoln wrote the Gettysburg Address while traveling from Washington to Gettysburg on the back of an envelope.

2. Although irregular, we will consider your request.

3. Three cars were reported stolen by the Groveton police yesterday.

4. Using a Doppler ultrasound device, fetal heartbeats can be detected by the twelfth week of pregnancy.

5. Locked in a vault for fifty years, the owner of the jewels has decided to sell them.

ANSWERS

1. While traveling from Washington to Gettysburg, Abraham Lincoln wrote the Gettysburg Address on the back of an envelope.

2. Although your request is irregular, we will consider it.

3. Yesterday the Groveton police reported the theft of three cars.

4. Using a Doppler ultrasound device, doctors can detect fetal heartbeats by the twelfth week of pregnancy.

5. The owner of the jewels that were locked in a vault for fifty years has decided to sell them.

Is It Okay to Occasionally Split an Infinitive?

A split infinitive occurs when an adverb or adverbial construction is placed between *to* and a verb: "to better understand"; "to always disagree" In a famous *New Yorker* cartoon, we see Captain Bligh sailing away from the *Bounty* in a rowboat and shouting, "So, Mr. Christian! You propose to unceremoniously cast me adrift?" The caption beneath the drawing reads: "The crew can no longer tolerate Captain Bligh's ruthless splitting of infinitives."

No reputable authority on usage, either in England or in the United States, bans the cleft infinitive. Good writers—Sir Philip Sidney, John Donne, Samuel Pepys, Samuel Johnson, George Eliot, Matthew Arnold, Thomas Hardy, Benjamin Franklin, Abraham Lincoln, Oliver Wendell Holmes, Emily Dickinson, and Henry James, to name a dozen out of thousands—have been splitting infinitives ever since the early fourteenth century, long before science learned how to split the atom.

Writers George Bernard Shaw and James Thurber were stylistically hassled by certain know-it-alls once too often. Shaw struck back in a letter to the *Times* of London: "There is a busybody on your staff who devotes a lot of time to chasing split infinitives. . . . I call for the immediate dismissal of this pedant. It is of no consequence whether he decides to go quickly or to quickly go or quickly to go. The important thing is that he should go at once." With typical precision and concision, Thurber wrote to a meddlesome editor, "When I split an infinitive, it is going to damn well stay split!"

Many so-called rules of English grammar are founded on models in the classical languages. But there is no precedent in these languages for condemning the split infinitive because in Greek and Latin (and all the other Romance languages) the infinitive is a single word that is impossible to sever.

Why is the alleged syntactical sin of splitting infinitives committed with such frequency? Primarily because in modern English, adjectives and adverbs are usually placed directly before the words they modify, as in "She successfully completed the course." The same people who thunder against adverbs plunked down in the middle of infinitives remain strangely silent about other split expressions: "She has successfully completed the course" (split verb phrase). "She boasted of successfully completing the course" (split prepositional phrase). We hear no objections to such sentences because in English it is perfectly natural to place adverbial modifiers before verbs, including infinitive verbs.

It is acceptable, but not always desirable, to place a string of qualifying words between *to* and its verb in an infinitive. "The company plans to immediately, and with as little fanfare as possible, remove the product from the market" is not incorrect, but "The company plans to remove the product from the market immediately and with as little fanfare as possible" is preferred. In many instances, avoiding the split infinitive is almost impossible, as in "The chairman said he expects the company's net income to more than double this year." In that instance, "more than" can go no other place.

When we suggest that you relax about splitting infinitives, we are not, to slightly paraphrase *Star Trek*, telling you to boldly go where no one else has gone before. Several studies of modern literary and journalistic writing reveal that a majority of newspaper and magazine editors would accept a sentence using the words "to instantly trace" and that the infinitive is cleft in 19.8 percent of all instances where an adverb appears.

We do not advocate that you go about splitting infinitives promiscuously and artlessly. If the practice bothers some readers, why not eliminate as many splits from your writing as you can? But there is no point in mangling a sentence just to avoid a split infinitive. Good writers occasionally employ the construction to gain emphasis, to attain the most natural and effective word order, and to avoid ambiguity.

Should All Who Enter Abandon *Hopefully*?

Hopefully, this book is stimulating your thinking about usage rules. If the structure of the last sentence squeaks like chalk over the blackboard of your sensibilities, you are not alone.

Since the seventeenth century, *hopefully* has been employed with the meaning "in a hopeful manner," as in Robert Louis Stevenson's aphorism "To travel hopefully is better than to arrive." But during the last three decades in the United States *hopefully* has donned new clothes. Now we can scarcely get through a day without meeting statements like "Hopefully, the changes taking place in Eastern Europe will make a safer world for our children" and "Her first day on the job will hopefully not be her last."

Something has happened to *hopefully* in such sentences. First, the adverb has acquired a new meaning, roughly "it is to be hoped." Second, *hopefully* now applies to situations (as in the two examples above) rather than only to people. Third, rather than modifying a specific verb (like *travel* in Stevenson's pronouncement), the adverb now modifies the entire sentence.

This highly fashionable (some would say *pandemic*) use of *hopefully* has provoked a ringing call to arms among protectors of the English language. The honor of being the first to cry out against the dangers of using *hopefully* as a floating adverb seems to belong to Wilson Follett, in *Modern American Usage*: "The special badness of *hopefully* is not alone that it strains *-ly* to the breaking point, but that it appeals to speakers and writers who do not think about what they are saying and pick up vogue words by reflex action."

Well, well. Let's now take a deep breath and, as we have been doing, examine structure and actual use. That *hopefully* has taken on a new meaning in no way disqualifies it from respectful consideration. Almost all English nouns, verbs, and modifiers have acquired meanings that they did not possess at birth. *Silly* once meant "blessed" and *awful* "full of awe," while words such as *knight*, once "a boy," and *governor*, once a "steersman or pilot," have come up in the world. Look what has happened recently to words such as *hip, energy,* and *grass*. When words like *hopefully* stop sparking off new meanings, our language, and probably we ourselves, will have died. The fact is that, except for a few diehard dictionaries, all contemporary lexicons accept "it is hoped" as a primary meaning of the adverb *hopefully.*

Now go back three paragraphs. Did you wince at our use of *first, second,* and *third* to kick off each sentence? That would be odd indeed; almost every speaker of English uses these adverbs as introducers. And what about these sentences?:

Mercifully, the war will soon be ended.

Apparently, the war will soon be ended.

Fortunately, the war will soon be ended.

Surely, the war will soon be ended.

Few English speakers would criticize the architecture of such sentences, yet each begins with an adverb that modifies the entire main clause. Why among all so-called floating adverbs in our language—*apparently, evidently, first* (*second* and *third* and so on), *fortunately, happily, however, luckily, mercifully, nevertheless, obviously, presumably, primarily, surely, thankfully, therefore, thus,* and umpteen other unexceptional expressions—should *hopefully* be singled out for condemnation?

The reason is that *hopefully* has become the "Have a nice day" of adverbs. Float your *hopefully*s too often and you will come across as a vacuous smiley face. The light's on, but—knock, knock—is anybody home? Hopefully, you understand our reservations about *hopefully*. Even better: We hope you understand our reservations about *hopefully*.

Should You Feel Bad about *Feeling Badly*?

Joining *hopefully* in the list of most vilified usages that we hear about most frequently from readers is the sentence "I feel badly." Syndicated columnist Michael Gartner states the classic view:

> Avoid the expression "I feel badly." Use "I feel bad." *Feel*, as you'd know if you had had Miss Hall in seventh grade, is a linking or, if you'll pardon the expression, copulative verb. These verbs take the adjectival form of modifiers (*bad*), not the adverbial form (*badly*).

Ask the offended why they object to "I feel badly," and the voices will slip into the tonal groove that the explanation has worn for itself: "If you feel badly, then your fingertips must have been cut off."

Here we confront the triumph of autocratic decree over reality, of mummified code over usage that actually inhales and exhales. In English, it is context, not form, that determines part of speech: That a word such as *badly* ends with *-ly* does not make it an immutable adverb modifying an action verb. Although a great many adverbs do indeed wag *-ly* tails, more than a hundred adjectives do too, among them *costly, deathly, elderly, fatherly, friendly, goodly, kindly, leisurely, manly, miserly, shapely, sickly,* and *worldly*.

Just as there are clear and important differences between the adjectives *sick* ("sick at this time") and *sickly* ("chronically sick") and *kind* ("kind at this moment") and *kindly* ("habitually kind"), a distinction is gradually gaining currency in our speech and writing between "I feel bad," meaning "I feel ill," and "I feel badly," meaning "I regret," "I'm sorry." In English, we have long used "I feel well" and "I feel good" to signal the difference between "I feel healthy" and "I feel happy." Is it not, then, natural that speakers and writers should want to distinguish between physical and mental ill-being as well as physical and mental well-being? Such a change pulls up a shade, opens a window in the house of language, and lets in the sunshine of a new nuance.

For the present, we advise that you do not write "I feel badly." For one thing, *badly* is not a fully assimilated adjective: The man who is sickly is a sickly man, but a person who feels badly can't be a badly person. For another thing, some readers will actually think that people who feel badly *are* having trouble with their fingertips.

We recommend that at this point in time, at this point, at this time, and now, you should feel bad, not badly.

Is *Alright* All Right?

Although rarer than *all right*, *alright* does appear in student and professional writing, newspaper and magazine advertisements, and in most modern dictionaries, including computer spell-checkers.

Experienced students of language know that usage ultimately determines meaning and spelling. *Minuscule*, for example, was for such a long time misspelled that *miniscule* was eventually entered in dictionaries as a variant and perfectly acceptable spelling. But our sense is that *alright* is a rather informal variant, probably influenced by *already* and *altogether*. Because these words are adverbs, while *all right* is an adjective, and because *alright* is going to raise the eyebrows of some of your readers and interfere with your achieving full communication, we recommend that you avoid *alright* altogether.

While we're putting our *all* into this section, let's consider a few other all-American modifiers:

All ready means "everybody or everything ready," while *already* is an adverb of time meaning "previously." If you could use the word *ready* alone, without changing the meaning of the sentence, *all ready* is the correct choice:

> After some initial anxiety, we were *all ready* to take the bus to the SAT center.

> They had *already* been to overnight camp for three weeks.

All together and *altogether* are similar to *all ready* and *already.* If you could use the word *together* by itself, write *all together.* If the meaning you seek is "thoroughly," write *altogether*:

> At the company picnic, the CEO, the secretaries, and the mailroom clerks, pulled *all together* on the rope. Their tug-of-war victory was an *altogether* satisfying experience.

Wise Words about *Wise*

Until the 1940s, the attachment of -*wise* to nouns and adjectives to form adverbs was limited to a relatively few well-established words, such as *likewise, otherwise, lengthwise, crosswise,* and *clockwise.* Then there began a mighty proliferation of -*wise* words, including *budgetwise, healthwise, saleswise,* and *weatherwise.*

Recognizing the increasing and nauseous overuse of the suffix, Adolph Goldsmith wrote a -*wise* parody of Hamlet's famous soliloquy:

> *To be or not to be: that is querywise:*
> *Whether 'tis nobler, mindwise, to suffer,*
> *Outrageous fortunewise, the slings and arrows,*
> *Or to take arms against troubles seawise,*
> *And oppositionwise to end them?*

In favor of the suffix, one can argue that *-wise* is a handy little word part because it economically circumvents such phrases as "in the manner of" and "in respect to." Moreover, *-wise* is the only way in English that we can convert a noun into an adverb.

But *-wise* has become so painfully overworked by politicians, sociologists, adsters, and sports figures that it offends sensitive eyes and ears. *-Wise* is an emblem of the kind of linguistic conformity that impoverishes the language by destroying variety:

- "Fabric-wise, I like this room best." —Lady Bird Johnson
- "The ballet goers see lively, leaping girls and boys whirling over the stage Americanwise." —London *Tatler*
- "We are not micromanaging Grenada intelligencewise until about that time frame." —Admiral Wesley L. McDonald
- "Alex Comfort's *Come Out and Play* may not be the most accomplished of books, constructionwise, but . . ." — London *Spectator*
- Shapewise, I feel good. —Earvin "Magic" Johnson

In the film *The Apartment*, Jack Lemmon says with a sigh, "That's the way it crumbles, cookiewise." Avoid this creeping suffix and your writing will not crumble, grammarwise.

The One and Only

The placement of the modifier *only* is one of the trickiest procedures in English usage. The most famous example of its vagaries is the song title "I Only Have Eyes for You." Formalists argue that the *only* is mislocated in this title and that the statement misleadingly implies "I have eyes—but no ears, nose, or mouth—for you," rather than "I have eyes for you—and nobody else but you." They insist that *only*—like *hardly, nearly, almost, scarcely, even*, and *just*— must appear right before the word modified, as in "I Have Eyes for Only You."

In reality no intelligent listener or reader would misinterpret the song line "I only have eyes for you." When *only* comes early in such a statement, the listener or reader is forewarned that the qualifier may be attached to almost any word that follows, and it is usually clear what that word is.

It may be that such a visualizing of the whole sentence is too much to ask of any speaker, but when equally natural placements of the modifier *only* are available, a writer should put the adjective or adverb immediately before the noun or verb it modifies.

Have we settled the issue of *only* once and for all? God only knows. Or maybe that should be: Only God knows.

TEST YOURSELF

The following statements are taken from newspapers, magazines, and a hotel room. Improve the sense by relocating the stray modifiers.

1. The FAA, however, only counts delays caused by weather and flight control.

2. The public only sees us on the track, and they probably don't recognize us in civilian clothes.

3. Due to the fluctuating price of silver, we can only guarantee the price of the coins for 10 days.

4. The Doors only produced one great album—their first—and their most indelible song, "Light My Fire," was written by guitarist Robby Krieger.

5. During your stay, this Refreshment Center will be restocked daily. You will only be charged for what you use.

ANSWERS

1. The FAA, however, counts only delays caused by weather and flight control.

2. The public sees us only on the track, and they probably don't recognize us in civilian clothes.

3. Due to the fluctuating price of silver, we can guarantee the price of the coins for only 10 days.

4. The Doors produced only one great album—their first—and their most indelible song,"Light My Fire," was written by guitarist Robby Krieger.

5. During your stay, this Refreshment Center will be restocked daily. You will be charged only for what you use.

Illogical Comparisons

On the airwaves you are constantly bombarded with claims such as "Our car is better than any car on the market." The ad is a logically impossible statement because the car in question can't be better than itself, and it is on the market. Similarly, "Michael Jordan is better than any basketball player in the history of the game" is true only if His Airness is not a basketball player. And when you read on an Orville Redenbacher popcorn package, "Do one thing, and do it better than anyone," you become paralyzed with inaction because, as a human being, you are an anyone, and you can't exceed yourself. "Any other car," "any other basketball player," and "anyone else" would clear up the confusions.

Writers owe it to their readers to make clear, complete, and logical comparisons. They must avoid confusing their readers by creating elliptical clauses of comparison that have two meanings. "Throckmorton likes golf more than his wife" should be rephrased as "Throckmorton likes golf more than his wife does" or "Throckmorton likes golf more than he likes his wife," depending on the writer's intention.

Another type of reader-unfriendly comparison involves a yoking together of two things that are not comparable. There must be a rational basis of comparison. In the sentence "The amateur gardener was elated when he produced more vegetables than his experienced neighbor's garden," the writer is awkwardly comparing a gardener to a garden. These sentences should be revised to compare apples with apples or oranges with oranges—in this case, person with person or garden with garden: "The amateur gardener was elated when he produced more vegetables than his neighbor" or "The amateur gardener was elated when his garden produced more vegetables than that of his experienced neighbor."

TEST YOURSELF

Repair the faulty comparisons in the following sentences:

1. Hi-Value Drugstore fills more prescriptions than any store in the Southeast.

2. At times, Uranus is farther away from the sun than Pluto.

3. My serve is even more thunderous than Pete Sampras.

4. Sergei Bubka has vaulted higher than anyone in the world.

5. The coach taught me more than the older players.

ANSWERS

1. Hi-Value Drugstore fills more prescriptions than any other store in the Southeast.

2. At times, Uranus is farther away from the sun than Pluto is. Or (but doubtful): At times, Uranus is farther away from the sun than it is from Pluto.

3. My serve is even more thunderous than Pete Sampras's.

4. Sergei Bubka has vaulted higher than anyone else in the world.

5. The coach taught me more than the older players taught me. Or: The coach taught me more than he taught the older players.

□ **15** □

Don't Miss Your Links

A generation ago, the airwaves were filled with a little jingle that twanged, "Winston tastes good like a cigarette should." English teachers and other word-watchers raised such a fuss about the use of *like* as a conjunction rather than a preposition that the publicity was worth millions to the Winston people.

Prepositions join nouns and pronouns to the rest of the sentence:

At that moment, the man *with* one leg *in* a cast hopped *onto* the train.

Conjunctions do just what the *Schoolhouse Rock* song says they do: "Conjunction, junction, what's your function? Hookin' up words and phrases and clauses":

She was too frightened to go up in a Ferris wheel; *but* when she scaled a rock face, she experienced both calm *and* ecstasy.

Prepositions and conjunctions are the glue words of language. These little joiners are not the most romantic of words, but they are among the most frequently used in our language. They also spark some of the most heated debates among grammarians, teachers, and writers:

Is It Okay to Use a Preposition to End a Sentence With?

Often a yawning chasm stretches between the so-called rules of usage and the English language in action. A clear instance of this gulf is the use of preposition to end a sentence. In truth, the greatest writers in English have freely ended sentences with prepositions. Why? Because the construction is a natural and graceful part of our English idiom. Here are a few examples from the masters:

- "Fly to others that we know not of"
  —William Shakespeare

- "We are such stuff / As dreams are made on."
  —William Shakespeare

- "Houses are built to live in, not to look on."
  —Francis Bacon

- "What a fine conformity would it starch us all into."
  —John Milton

- . . . soil good to be born on, good to live on, good to die for, and to be buried in."
  —James Russell Lowell

- "All words are pegs to hang ideas on."
  —Henry Ward Beecher

- "Give me a kiss to build a dream on."
  —line from a popular song

The final preposition is one of the glories of the English language. If we shackle its idioms and muffle its music with false rules, we diminish the power of our language. If we rewrite the quotations above to conform to the rule against terminal prepositions, the natural beauty of our prose and verse is forced to bow before a stiff bureaucratic code of structure: "Fly to others of whom we know not"; "All words are pegs upon which to hang ideas"; "Give me a kiss on which to build a dream." Now the statements are artificial—people simply don't talk and write like that—and, in most cases, wordier. A preposition following a verb usually has an adverbial function as well, so that it is normal and natural to want to keep verb and preposition together in the sentence.

The most widely circulated tale of the terminal preposition involves Sir Winston Churchill, one of the greatest of all English prose stylists. As the story goes, a Whitehall editor had the audacity to "correct" a proof of Churchill's memoirs by revising a sentence that ended with the outlawed preposition. Sir Winston hurled back at the proofreader a memorable rebuttal: "This is the kind of impertinence up with which I will not put!"

A variation on this story concerns a newspaper columnist who responded snappily to the accusation that he was uncouthly violating the terminal preposition "rule":

> What do you take me for? A chap who doesn't know how to make full use of all the easy variety the English language is capable of? Don't you know that ending a sentence with a preposition is an idiom many famous writers are very fond of? They realize it's a colloquialism a skillful writer can do a great deal with. Certainly it's a linguistic device you ought to read about.

For the punster there's the setup joke about the prisoner who asked a female guard to marry him on the condition that she help him escape. He used a preposition to end a sentence with.

Our favorite of all terminal preposition stories involves a boy attending public school and one attending private school who happen to be sitting next to each other in an airplane. To be friendly, the public schooler turns to the preppie and asks, "What school are you at?"

The private schooler looks down his aquiline nose at the public school student and comments, "I happen to attend an institution at which we are taught to know better than to conclude sentences with prepositions."

The boy at public school pauses for a moment and then says: "All right, then. What school are you at, dingbat!" (Expletive replaced.)

We recommend that you terminate sentences with prepositions when they offer useful emphasis and create natural language. But don't use them gratuitously, as in the heading to this section of the chapter. "Is It Okay to Use a Preposition to End a Sentence?" is better; the *With* is superfluous.

And Is It Okay to Use a Conjunction to Begin a Sentence?

The grammar cop who issues you a ticket for starting sentences with *and* and *but* may be the same self-appointed officer who informs you that you should never split an infinitive or terminate a sentence prepositionally. But, as Wilson Follett explains in *Modern American Usage*, "A prejudice lingers from the days of school-marmish rhetoric that a sentence should not begin with *and*. The supposed rule is without foundation in grammar, logic, or art. . . . The false rule used to apply to *but* equally; it is now happily forgotten." Various studies indicate that many professional writers begin one tenth of their sentences with coordinate conjunctions.

The *Oxford English Dictionary* offers examples, ranging from the tenth to the nineteenth century, of coordinating conjunctions kicking off sentences. The Bible is full of them—"And God saw that it was good"—as is the book you are reading. We, your reader-friendly authors, use whatever tools the English language offers to express our views and serve the rhythm of our sentences. So should you, as we just did in the final paragraph of the section preceding this one.

TEST YOURSELF

Sometimes writers incorrectly use a comma to replace a conjunction or an adverb. Two sentences written as one, with only a comma between them, are called comma splices or run-on sentences.

In the statements that follow, identify those that are grammatically correct and those that are comma-spliced. Rewire the spliced examples.

1. Robert Burns was not always a great man, however, he was a truly great poet.

2. Old Mr. Gray loved all his grandchildren, but Agatha was his pride and joy.

3. She is a talented writer, in fact, she is a genius.

4. It was Sunday night, and hundreds of hotel guests were checking in and out.

5. Natasha took a sip of vodka and pushed back her chair, then she began to laugh.

ANSWERS

1. Robert Burns was not always a great man; however, he was a truly great poet. Or the sentence could be written as ". . . man. However, ..." *However* is a conjunctive adverb that should not join independent clauses.

2. Correct. *But* is a coordinating conjunction.

3. She is a talented writer; in fact, she is a genius. Or: ". . . writer. In fact, . . ." *In fact* is an adverbial prepositional phrase that should not connect independent clauses.

4. Correct. *And* is a coordinating conjunction.

5. Natasha took a sip of vodka and pushed back her chair; then she began to laugh. Or: ". . . chair. Then . . ." *Then* is an adverb and should not link independent clauses.

A *Like*-ly Story

The "Winston tastes good" commercials garnered so much free press and air time that the cigarette hucksters came back with a second campaign: "What do you want—good grammar or good taste?" We're not sure about the taste, but, for most educated Americans, the use of *like* in the Winston commercial contains good grammar (really, good usage).

Among prescriptive grammarians the prevailing rule is that we may use *like* or *as* as a preposition joining a noun to an earlier word—"cleans like a white tornado," "blind as a bat"—but we must not use *like* as a conjunction that introduces an adverb clause. Thus, the son-of-Winston commercial slogan "Nobody can do it like McDonald's can" is unacceptable to them because the sentence doesn't sound good like a conjunction should.

Even princes have been royally reprimanded for violating this admonition. Back in the nineteenth century the poet laureat Alfred, Lord Tennyson told the linguist F. J. Furnivall, "It's a modern vulgarism that I have seen grow up within the past thirty years; and when Prince Albert used it in my drawing room, I pulled him up for it, in the presence of the Queen, and told him he never ought to use it again."

But any open-minded, open-eared observer of the living English language cannot fail to notice that tens of everyday expressions employ *like* as a subordinating conjunction. Fill in the following blanks: "He tells it _____ it is"; "She ate _____ there was no tomorrow"; "If you knew Suzie _____ I know Suzie . . ."; "Let's all sing _____ the birdies sing"; "They make the food here just _____ my mother used to." And what about "Winston tastes good _____ a cigarette should" and "Nobody can do it _____ McDonald's can"? We are confident that, despite the fact that each blank kicks off an adverb clause, most native English speakers would naturally supply *like*.

Again we advise you to gauge your audience, and choose between *like* and *as*. The more formal the context and the more puristic your audience, the more likely you are to select *as*, *as if*, and *as though* from your tool kit to join a subordinate clause to the rest of the sentence. If we're wrong, then we don't know our *as* from a hole in the ground.

TEST YOURSELF

How strong is your grasp of the grammar, usage, spelling, and punctuation presented in the past eight chapters of this book? To help you find out, here's a passage marred by more than thirty goofs that are frequently found in print. How many can you catch and correct?

Sad Day in the Classroom

"I sincerely feel like you students should have passed the test," lamented the teacher who obviously felt badly about the whole affair. Each student in the class refused to except the fact that they had failed, but the teacher was one of those pedagogues who was a tough grader.

Jack was an obvious choice as class spokesman, although he would of gone along with whomever else was chosen. Mary's situation was different than Jack. Her class standing was more effected by the grade because she had answered less questions correctly. Trying hard to answer rationally, the reply Mary offered was "This test is harder and longer then any I have taken. Can you tell us what the test was about and your purpose in giving it?"

The teacher answered, "If I was in you're place, I too would be upset." The class was impressed by the teacher trying to explain his position so clearly, nevertheless, it seemed to them that, in their opinion, the teacher should not have taken points off for spelling. An extremely nit-picking approach.

Neither Mary or the other members of the class was in a position to disagree strongly with the teacher, although they could not help but scarcely feel that they knew more about fairness than him.

Now that everyone had lain their cards on the table, the teacher preceded to explain how important it was to be experienced and how much the students lacked it. "Please do not imply," he added, "that it is all together easy to insure fairness on tests."

--- ANSWERS ---

"I sincerely feel **that** [*like* is usually a preposition and, in this case, awkwardly introduces the noun clause; *as if* is also acceptable] you students should have passed the test," lamented the teacher, [comma before restrictive clause] who obviously felt **bad** [it's risky to use *badly* as a predicate adjective] about the whole affair. **The students** in the class refused to **accept** the fact that they [pluralize to avoid sexism and awkwardness] had failed, but the teacher was one of those pedagogues **who were tough graders**. [The adjective clause modifies *pedagogues*, not *one*.]

Jack was an obvious choice as class spokesman, although he would **have** gone along with **whoever** [*whoever* is the subject of the passive verb *was chosen*] else was chosen. Mary's situation was different **from Jack's** [*different from* before nouns; illogical comparison]. Her class standing was more **affected** by the grade because she had answered **fewer** [*fewer* for countable entities] questions correctly. Trying hard to answer rationally, Mary **replied**, [dangling participle] "This test is harder and longer **than** any **other** [illogical comparison] I have taken. Can you tell us what the test was about and **why you gave it** [faulty parallelism]?"

The teacher answered, "If I **were** [subjunctive mood for condition contrary to fact] in **your** place, I too would be upset." The class was impressed by the **teacher's** [possessive noun before gerund object] trying to explain his position so clearly. **Nevertheless** [avoid a comma splice], it seemed to them that [*in their opinion* is redundant] the teacher should not have taken points off for spelling, **an** extremely nitpicking approach [sentence fragment].

Neither Mary **nor** the other members of the class **were** [with *nor* the verb must agree with the nearer subject] in a position to disagree strongly with the teacher, although they could not help but [*scarcely* generates a double negative] feel that they knew more about fairness than **he** [subject of understood verb *did*].

Now that **they all** had **laid their** [pluralize to avoid sexism and awkwardness] cards on the table, the teacher **proceeded** to explain how important **experience is** and how much the students lacked **that experience** [vague pronoun reference]. "Please do not **infer**," he added, "that it is **altogether** easy to **ensure** fairness on tests."

□ 16 □

A Spell of Good English

For generations, business executives, teachers, and other professionals have complained about the poor English produced by their employees and students. Often what they mean by poor English is poor spelling, since errors in orthography are the most conspicuous of all defects in written English.

Two of the words spelled *spell*—the noun *spell*, meaning "a magical incantation," and the verb *spell*, meaning "to place the letters of a word in proper order"—are historically related. Both grow from an Indo-European root that means "to say aloud, to recite."

As a writer, you may indeed feel spellbound, entangled in a letter-web of words inhabited by creepy, crawly creatures. Confronted by what linguist Mario Pei calls "the awesome mess of English spelling," you may well wonder if you can ever become a better speller. We believe that you can, especially if you imbibe six handy and relatively painless home remedies:

1. Identify the particular spelling demons that torment you. Tape a list of these demons to your desk or your bathroom mirror. Review them frequently and you will make progress. Remember that even the worst spellers write far more words correctly than they misspell. The number of words that cause writers trouble is relatively small, and they tend to be the common words. According to a number of studies, the most frequently misspelled words and word groups are:

(1) *there/their/they're*

(2) *to/too/two*

(3) *receive*

(4) *existence/existent*

(5) *occur/occurred/occurrence/occurring*

(6) *definite/definitely/definition*

(7) *separate/separation*

(8) *belief/believe*

(9) *occasion/occasional*

(10) *lose/losing*

2. ***Own a reliable and up-to-date desk dictionary and use it constantly.*** As soon as a misspelled word comes to your attention, look up the correct spelling. The average time for locating a word in the dictionary is twenty seconds, surely twenty seconds well spent.

3. ***Look for patterns.*** Despite its apparent chaos, much of English spelling makes sense. As we pointed out earlier, two words that are frequently interchanged are *stationary,* "not moving," and *stationery,* "writing paper." Yet there exists a reasonable distinction between them: *-ary* is characteristically an adjective ending, as in *ordinary* and *military,* whereas *-ery* is just as typically a noun ending, as in *machinery* and *mystery.* As you become more aware of such patterns, you will easily distinguish the adjectives *ingenious* and *callous* from the nouns *genius* and *callus*.

4. *Think of words as made up of component parts*. The old saying "It's hard by the yard but a cinch by the inch" applies to spelling as well as other matters. The common misspellings of *misspelling* (often *mispelling*) and *disappoint* (often *dissapoint*) are caused by a failure to perceive the prefix-root components of these words: *mis + spelling* and *dis + appoint*. Other examples:

back	+	ground	=	*background*
dis	+	satisfied	=	*dissatisfied*
pre	+	judice	=	*prejudice*
re	+	commend	=	*recommend*
room	+	mate	=	*roommate*
un	+	necessary	=	*unnecessary*
with	+	hold	=	*withhold*

5. *Learn and apply a relatively small number of spelling rules*, each of which pertains to a large cache of words:

(a) Words ending in *y* preceded by a consonant usually change the *y* to *i* before a suffix not beginning with *i*, as in *cry-cried*, *baby-babies*, *busy-business*, and *beauty-beautiful*.

(b) Drop the final *e* before adding a suffix beginning with a vowel, as in *dine-dining*, *hope-hoping*, *desire-desirable*, *orate-oratory*. Exceptions: *ce* and *ge* before *a* or *o* do not drop their *e*, in order to retain their soft sound, as in *serviceable*, *singeing*, and *outrageous*. Note that the pairings *love-lovely*, *nine-ninety*, and *state-statement* retain the final *e*, because the suffixes begin with consonants.

(c) Write *i* before *e*,
    Except after *c*,
    Or when sounded as *ay*,
    As in *neighbor* and *weigh*.

Exceptions to this rule abound—*either*, *leisure*, and *financier* come to mind—but most *ie-ei* words adhere to the pattern, including the gremlins *achieve, believe, ceiling, niece,* and *receive.*

(d) Now take a breath and learn the toughest but most useful spelling rule in English:

Words ending in a single consonant preceded by a single vowel double the final consonant before a suffix beginning with a vowel if the accent falls on the last syllable of the root word.

Whew! It takes a lungful of words to recite this rule, but the application is easy:

> *hop-hopping,* but *hope-hoping* (*hope* falls within rule *b,* above)

> *pin-pinning,* but *pine-pining* (*pine* falls within rule *b,* above)

> *pet-petting* but *carpet-carpeting* (the accent in *carpet* falls on the first, not the second, syllable)

> *refer-referred,* but *reference* (the accent in *reference* falls on the first syllable)

6. *Use mnemonic devices to subdue your spelling demons.*
A mnemonic device is a memory aid that may work for you where other strategies fail. The following memory tricks may help you to exorcize some of your most bedeviling (not bedevilling) spelling demons:

> **all right.** *All right* is the opposite of *all wrong.*

> **anoint.** Think of *an ointment* and you won't spell this word with a double *n.*

> **beautiful.** The only English word that ends in *full* is *full. Beautiful, wonderful,* and the like end in *-ful.*

> **business.** *Business* descends from *busyness.*

> **calendar.** Memorize this sentence to help you tame the demons ending in *-ar:* "The *particular burglar* and *beggar* took only a *grammar* book, *calendar,* and a *sugar* bowl."

> **cemetery.** Note that almost every other letter is an *e.*

> **conscience.** There is *science* in *conscience.*

definite.   Something that is *definite* has *finite* boundaries.

desert-dessert.   You want no more than one *desert*. Hence, one *s*. You want more than one *dessert*. Hence, two *s*'s.

despair.   Remember that this word starts with the same four letters as *desperate*.

environment.   There is *iron* in the *environment*.

forty.   It is strange that *forty* drops the *u* that appears in *four*. You'll have no problem, though, if you memorize the sentence "The soldiers built a *fort forty* yards from the clearing."

grammar.   *Ma* wants you to use good grammar. She also wants you to remember that the letters after the *g* read the same forwards and backwards.

lose.   *Lose* loses an *o* from *loose*.

minuscule.   You get a *minus* if you don't use the preferred spelling of *minuscule*.

parallel.   The two *l*'s make parallel lines in the middle of *parallel*.

piece.   You'll not experience an unwelcome vowel movement if you remember "I want a *piece* of pie."

prejudice.   This word begins with the same six letters as *prejudge*.

principal-principle.   The *principal* is your *pal*. A *principle* is a rule that ends with the same two letters as *rule*. Let the *a* in *principal* remind you that *principal* can also be an adjective.

recognize.   There is a *cog* in *recognize*.

repetition.   There is a *pet* in *repetition*. Just place *re-* before *petition*.

rhythm.   If you've got it but can't spell it, divide *rhythm* into two three-letter syllables, each having an *h* in the middle.

ridiculous. The adjective begins with the same seven letters as *ridicule*.

secretary. A *secretary* keeps *secrets*. To master the demons that end in *-ary*, memorize this sentence: "The *stationary secretary* earned a raise in *salary* for using a *dictionary*."

sentence. Count *ten* before you write *sentence*.

separate. There is *a rat* in *separate*.

stationary-stationery. Something that is *stationary* is standing. Remember the *a* in *stand*. *Stationery* stores sell *letter paper*. Remember the *er*'s in *letter paper*.

We think of a good speller as a freckle-faced kid who reels off the letters in *eleemosynary* and *hippopotomonstrosesquipedalian* at the state spelling bee. But the good speller is also you, who have enough sense to memorize fifty to a hundred demons, to learn a small number of fundamental spelling rules and mnemonic devices, and to own and consult frequently a reputable and up-to-date dictionary of the English language.

Test Yourself

Here is a list of one hundred demonic demons. In each pair one version is the correct spelling, and the other is the most common misspelling. Within each duo, circle the one you trust. If you score 50 or below, consider yourself exceedingly unlucky. If your total is 51–60, you are orthographically challenged, while 61–75 is average. You are above average if you can nail 75–85 and superior if you can circle 86 or more proper forms.

1. abcess, abscess
2. acadamy, academy
3. accommodate, accomodate
4. accross, across
5. acheive, achieve
6. accordian, accordion
7. aggressive, agressive
8. analagy, analogy
9. anialate, annihilate
10. annoint, anoint

11. arctic, artic
12. asinine, assinine
13. athalete, athlete
14. background, backround
15. banana, bannana
16. basically, basicly
17. battalion, battallion
18. benefit, benifit
19. beautiful, beautyfull
20. boundary, boundry
21. broccoli, brocoli
22. business, busness
23. candadate, candidate
24. calandar, calendar
25. cantalope, cantaloupe
26. caracature, caricature
27. casette, cassette
28. catagory, category
29. ceiling, cieling
30. cemetary, cemetery
31. challange, challenge
32. charactar, character
33. cheif, chief
34. choclate, chocolate
35. commitee, committee
36. commitment, committment
37. complection, complexion
38. contraversy, controversy
39. curiosity, curiousity
40. definate, definite
41. description, discription
42. despair, dispair
43. develop, develope
44. dilema, dilemma
45. disappoint, dissapoint
46. ecstasy, exstasy
47. embarass, embarrass
48. environment, enviroment
49. exhilarated, exilerated

50. existance, existence
51. forty, fourty
52. grammar, grammer
53. harass, harrass
54. hypocricy, hypocrisy
55. imediate, immediate
56. inate, innate
57. independant, independent
58. ingenious, ingenius
59. innoculate, inoculate
60. judgement, judgment
61. marshmallow, marshmellow
62. metaphor, metaphore
63. millenium, millennium
64. mischievious, mischievous
65. mispelled, misspelled
66. missile, missle
67. mocassin, moccasin
68. noticeable, noticable
69. occasion, occassion
70. occurrance, occurrence
71. pastime, pasttime
72. parallel, parralel
73. perseverance, perseverence
74. pharaoh, pharoah
75. pizzaria, pizzeria
76. poinsettia, pointsettia
77. precede, preceed
78. predjudice, prejudice
79. priviledge, privilege
80. procede, proceed
81. publically, publicly
82. receive, recieve
83. reccommend, recommend
84. renoun, renown
85. repetition, repitition
86. rhythm, rithim
87. roomate, roommate
88. sacreligious, sacrilegious

89. sentance, sentence
90. separate, seperate
91. silhouette, sillouette
92. sophmore, sophomore
93. subtlely, subtly
94. supercede, supersede

95. suprise, surprise
96. threshhold, threshold
97. tradgedy, tragedy
98. truely, truly
99. tyranny, tyrrany
100. unecessary, unnecessary

ANSWERS

1. abscess	27. cassette	53. harass	77. precede
2. academy	28. category	54. hypocrisy	78. prejudice
3. accommodate	29. ceiling	55. immediate	79. privilege
4. across	30. cemetery	56. innate	80. proceed
5. achieve	31. challenge	57. independent	81. publicly
6. accordion	32. character	58. ingenious	82. receive
7. aggressive	33. chief	59. inoculate	83. recommend
8. analogy	34. chocolate	60. judgment is	84. renown
9. annihilate	35. committee	preferred in	85. repetition
10. anoint	36. commitment	the U.S.	86. rhythm
11. arctic	37. complexion	61. marshmallow	87. roommate
12. asinine	38. controversy	62. metaphor	88. sacrilegious
13. athlete	39. curiosity	63. millennium	89. sentence
14. background	40. definite	64. mischievous	90. separate
15. banana	41. description	65. misspelled	91. silhouette
16. basically	42. despair	66. missile	92. sophomore
17. battalion	43. develop	67. moccasin	93. subtly
18. benefit	44. dilemma	68. noticeable	94. supersede
19. beautiful	45. disappoint	69. occasion	95. surprise
20. boundary	46. ecstasy	70. occurrence	96. threshold
21. broccoli	47. embarrass	71. pastime	97. tragedy
22. business	48. environment	72. parallel	98. truly
23. candidate	49. exhilarated	73. perseverance	99. tyranny
24. calendar	50. existence	74. pharaoh	100. unnecessary
25. cantaloupe	51. forty	75. pizzeria	
26. caricature	52. grammar	76. poinsettia	

□ 17 □

Don't Be Comma-tose

Of all the devices that make writing reader-friendly, none is more important than punctuation. Imagine if you can how reader-unfriendly writing would be with no punctuation at all.

Punctuation and capitalization are just as important as the words themselves in getting meaning across to your readers when you talk you do more than put your thoughts into words because words alone cannot express your thoughts exactly you raise and lower your voice and pause for varying lengths of time to indicate exactly which words are important and which are merely side remarks where phrases clauses and sentences begin and end and whether the sentence is a statement question or command the pauses and voice changes which you use without much conscious thought work with the words to make your meanings clear punctuation is for readers not writers when you write rather than speak you need punctuation marks to serve your readers in the same way that timing pitch and inflection serve your listeners in short the primary purpose of punctuation is to make reading easier by establishing relationships between and among the parts of your written statements by now it is clear to you how tortuous and torturous reading can be without punctuation

This chapter and the next discuss the main marks of punctuation and their uses. We designed this section of the book as a concise guide for writers who want to punctuate according to generally accepted standards. We'll start with the comma—the most frequently employed of all marks—and then cover (alphabetically) apostrophes, brackets, colons, dashes, ellipses, exclamation points, hyphens, parentheses, periods, question marks, quotation marks, and semicolons.

The most important function of a comma is to indicate a natural pause. If you use commas in that way, without bothering consciously to follow rules, you will not be wrong often. One problem with that approach, however, is that a pause that is natural to one reader is not necessarily natural to another. The play-it-by-ear approach tends to generate more commas than modern writers like to use and modern readers like to read.

Whether you strew commas through your sentences like confetti or plant them like precious seeds, singly and far from each other, a little time spent learning the accepted conventions will eliminate comma trauma from your life. To summarize the most important of these guidelines, we shall identify three functions that commas serve: joining, listing, and setting off.

Use commas before coordinating conjunctions to join two independent clauses. The coordinating conjunctions are *and, but, or, nor, yet, for,* and *so.* An independent clause is a subject-verb combination that expresses a complete thought and thus could stand alone:

> The company lost money last year, but management expects substantial earnings this year.

In compound sentences the comma is often omitted if

the two clauses are short and closely related, especially when the conjunction is *and* or *or*.

We've been discussing the joining of independent clauses. Do not use a comma before a conjunction joining a word, a phrase, or a subordinate clause:

> I don't care for broccoli or cauliflower.

> The rules of punctuation are important because they lend clarity and order to writing.

Use commas to list words, phrases, or clauses in a series of similar grammatical structures:

> The recipe for Kickapoo Joy Juice calls for formaldehyde, skunk oil, white lightning, and anything else you care to throw in.

> The flying saucer descended swiftly, hovered for a few minutes, and then disappeared into the night heavens.

> Down the mountain, over the river, and through the woods, to Grandmother's house I went.

Note that we have placed commas before each of the conjunctions that precede the last item in each series. This little mark is called the serial comma. Most newspapers and many other publications do not advocate using this serial comma, but in more formal writing, such as essays, business letters, and literary works like this book, the serial comma is ordinarily retained. We recommend the use of the serial comma because we have found that in many sentences the comma before the conjunction is an aid to clarity, emphasis, and meaning. Consider:

> For dinner, the Girl Scouts ate steak, onions and ice cream.

> For dinner, the Girl Scouts ate steak, onions, and ice cream.

> The serial comma is an aid to clarity, emphasis and meaning.

The serial comma is an aid to clarity, emphasis, and meaning.

What the soldier missed most about home were his dog, his little brother, the odor of his dad's pipe and his girlfriend.

The first sentence sounds as if the Scouts devoured a yucky concoction of onions and (urp!) ice cream; the serial comma in the second sentence avoids such gastronomic ambiguity. In the third sentence, the rhythm of the series sounds uneven, while the serial comma in the fourth helps the final term, *meaning*, to ring out as loudly as the others. The fifth sentence misspeaks for itself.

Use commas to list adjectives in a series if the adjectives are of equal importance. Another approach is to ask if you are using the commas in the sentence in place of *and*:

They live in a large, comfortable, well-designed house.

Do not use commas to list adjectives in a series if the adjectives seem so closely related as to form a single unit:

They live in a large two-story country house.

Use commas to set off introductory appositives, phrases, and clauses:

A fine scholar and athlete, Tony deserves admission to your college.

Mocking the hare, the tortoise crawled across the finish line.

After tortoise crossed the finish line, he offered the hare a course in time management.

Use commas to set off parenthetical words, conjunctive adverbs, nouns of direct address, and nonrestrictive appositives, phrases, and clauses:

Dr. Karloff will stay on, I suppose, until the research is completed.

The company, nevertheless, plans to introduce the product immediately.

Brother, can you pair a dime—with a dollar?

Vanessa Jensen, a mother of three, works in a department store.

Citizen Kane, made in 1941, often heads the list of the greatest American films.

Do you recall 1941, when the dark clouds of world war gathered on the horizon?

Use commas to set off complete quotations:

She lamented, "Clear writing is one of the skills we often find lacking in recent graduates."

Use commas to set off the year from the day of the month and the state from the city. Note that the commas after years and states are among the most underused marks of punctuation:

November 23, 1963, was a shattering day in many people's lives.

Kennett Square, Pennsylvania, is the mushroom capital of the United States.

Finally, we offer two last and crucial rules:

Use a comma whenever one will prevent confusion:

Hemingway did not, like Fitzgerald, sell his soul to Hollywood.

Whatever will be, will be.

Use commas to help communicate meaning. Because they indicate a short pause and relative minor emphasis, commas are more often considered optional than other marks of punctuation. Compare:

The master beat the scholar with a strap.

The master beat the scholar, with a strap.

According to Henry W. Fowler, the difference between the first and second versions is the gulf between matter-of-factness and indignation.

Punctuation is an art as well as a science. The marks you will study in the next chapter will provide you additional options to convey nuances of meaning and emphasis:

The master beat the scholar (with a strap).

The master beat the scholar: with a strap.

The master beat the scholar—with a strap.

□ 18 □

The Marks of Good Writing

Punctuation developed after writing, not along with it as we might suppose. Early writing had no breaks between words and no punctuation. Some early texts were *boustrophedon*, which means "as the ox draws the plow." The words in these texts went from left to right and from right to left in alternating lines, much as oxen pull plows and modern high-speed printers print a page. Readers were required not only to supply their own punctuation but also to read backward.

Fortunately, we who are writing and reading today have an army of punctuation marks arrayed against confusion and ready to clarify the messages we send and receive. Here are our punctilious soldiers, who will now parade before us alphabetically:

THE APOSTROPHE

Of all marks of punctuation the most off-putting is the apostrophe, so much so that people put apostrophes off when they should be putting them on paper and often put them on when they should be putting them off. Indeed, the dread diseases of apostrophlation (gratuitous apostrophes) and apostrophy (the atrophy of proper apostrophes) are sweeping across our land. In an effort to halt the spread of these plagues, we herewith present its (not it's) symptoms, along with a prescription for its cure.

First, some symptoms:

- A lavish television production repeatedly advertised the play it was presenting as "Charles Dicken's *Nicholas Nickleby.*" If Dicken were alive today, he'd be turning over in his grave.
- Teachers at Bellamy High School, in Chicopee, Massachusetts, received $25 from the Midas Muffler Company for spotting and reporting an apostrophe catastrophe on a large roadside billboard that read "It Pay's to Midasize."
- The erudite Harvard Club of Boston was crimson-faced to discover that one of its lavatories was labeled "Mens' Room."
- In the French market in New Orleans stand signs that announce "Pear's" and (gasp!) "Peach'es."
- In a weekly swap-sell guide published in Maine appeared this grisly (not grizzly or gristly) ad: "Wanted: guitar for college student to learn to play, classical non-electric, also piano to replace daughters lost in fire." Ah, the difference a lost apostrophe makes.

Here's the skinny on apostrophes:

Use apostrophes to form possessives. A *New Yorker* cartoon depicts a policeman pulling over to the side of the road a truck labeled "Me and Wallys Produce." The cop says to the driver, "Sorry, but I'm going to have to issue you a summons for reckless grammar and driving without an apostrophe." To make a singular noun possessive, add an apostrophe and *s*:

Wally's Produce   the policeman's badge   the boss's son

If two or more people own or share the same thing, use the apostrophe only after the name of the last one:

Ben and Jerry's ice cream company

Clinton and Gore's administration

But if the items are individually owned, use an apostrophe with each name or noun:

Ben's and Jerry's houses

Clinton's and Gore's home states

Grammarians and publications differ on forming the possessive of singular words ending in sibilants—*s*, *z*, *c*, or *x*. We recommend as the most sensible practice that you add the *s* after the apostrophe if you would pronounce that *s*.

To form the possessive of plural words that end in *s*, add only the apostrophe:

the Joneses' daughter   the readers' opinions

This is consistent with the rule we stated above for singular nouns ending in *s*. Pronunciation is the key. When you don't pronounce the possessives, don't write an *s* after the apostrophe. For a plural word that ends in a letter other than *s*, form the possessive as if the word were singular:

the people's choice   the men's room

This brings us to those placards we see on or in front of houses everywhere—The Smith's, The Gump's, and even (sigh) The Jone's. These are distressing signs of our times. Which Smith, we ask, and what is it that this Smith possesses? And who, pray tell, is Jone?

Who lives in the house? The Smiths. The Gumps. The Joneses. That's what the signs should say. If you must make a possessive statement, place the apostrophe after the plural names—The Smiths', The Gumps', The Joneses'. Your attention to this matter will strike a blow against the nationwide conspiracy of shop teachers and sign-makers dedicated to perpetrating and perpetuating apostrophe catastrophe throughout our land.

Remember, too, that possessive forms of personal pronouns, such as *yours*, *hers*, and *ours*, do not require the apostrophe. *It's* and *who's* are not possessives; they are contractions of *it is* or *it has* and *who is* or *who has*. Please, please do not use *it's* as a possessive.

Use apostrophes to show the omission of elements in a word:

I've   the fall of '95   finger lickin' good   four o'clock

Use apostrophes to form plurals of letters or numbers, or words when the apostrophes will prevent confusion:

How many *i*'s are there in *Mississippi*?

Here are the do's and don'ts of using apostrophes.

Where there is no confusion, don't use apostrophes for plurals:

1920s   the ABCs   his CDs

Test Yourself

Here's a quiz to help you to avoid apostrophe catastrophes. Insert apostrophes or apostrophes and *s*, where needed, into each of the items below:

1. the womans car
2. Gus mother
3. Jesus parables
4. Achilles wrath
5. the babies diapers
6. anyones guess
7. its paw
8. the 1990s
9. no ifs, ands, or buts
10. doesnt

─────────────── ANSWERS ───────────────

1. the woman's car

2.–4. Most of us say *Gus's*, and the punctuation should reflect the oral form of the word. To our ears, either *Jesus'* or *Jesus's* is acceptable, while *Achilles'* seems far more natural than the spluttering *Achilles's*.

5. If a plural noun ends with an *s* or *z* sound, add the apostrophe only—"the babies' diapers," "the Snaggles' house."

6.–7. Use the apostrophe and *s* for possessive impersonal pronouns, such as *anyone's* and *everybody's*, but never use the apostrophe and *s* for possessive pronouns, such as *its* and *yours*.

8.–9. Modern style favors a simple *s* for plurals, unless confusion would result.

10. Use the apostrophe to indicate contractions and other omissions—hence *doesn't*.

BRACKETS

Use brackets to insert a missing word or comment within a quotation:

> He was quoted as saying, "Tyson's left hook packs more punch than [Dempsey's] uppercut."

> What he actually wrote was: "These arguments [referring presumably to the assertions of his opponent] are entirely irrelevant to the present situation in Rwanda."

THE COLON

In his monumental *Modern English Usage*, the inestimable Henry W. Fowler wrote, self-referentially, that the colon has acquired a special function: that of "delivering goods that have been invoiced in the preceding words."

What are the "goods" that the colon delivers?

Use the colon to introduce a list, a long quotation, or a complete statement that explains or expands on immediately foregoing information:

I have three goals in life: to be healthy, to do useful work, and to leave the world a better place than I found it.

Wilson Follett has this to say about the colon: "The colon is used to introduce formally. It furnishes this service for lists, tables, and quotations, or for the second member of a two-sentence statement when the first raises an expectation or makes a promise to be fulfilled by the second."

Use of the colon is often a stylistic preference: Many writers like to use a colon in place of a period to show, as in this very sentence, that what follows is an illustration of what precedes.

One last introductory function of the colon is its appearance in letter writing. *Use a colon—never a semicolon, please!—after a salutation to introduce the body of a business letter*:

Dear Mr. Mergenthwerker: To Whom It May Concern:

THE DASH

Use dashes to interrupt the main thought of a sentence and to set off explanatory remarks. You might consider the dash as a strong comma most often used to convey an abrupt break in a sentence:

Wallingford's recent novel—his first attempt at fiction, you know—has been praised by most of the leading critics.

Dashes are one choice you have to introduce or set off a series less formally than using a colon:

For centuries, fair-haired sea rovers from North Germany—Angles, Saxons, and Jutes—habitually cruised the British coast in beaked Viking ships.

Use dashes to gather up the parts to an introductory series:

> The increasing use of the telephone, the pervasiveness of television, and the extraordinary availability of automobile and air travel—all these elements have contributed to a decline in the art of personal letter writing.

In *An American Rhetoric*, William W. Watt makes his (and our) opinion clear about another use of the dash: "The dash is also used as an all-purpose gadget by people dashing off letters and notes in too much of a hurry to punctuate. This promiscuous use of the dash can become an irritating nuisance when it occurs in writing more serious than chitchat between pen pals."

ELLIPSIS

An ellipsis is the intentional omission of a word or words. When a portion of a direct quotation is omitted, indicate the ellipsis by three periods (. . .) called an ellipsis mark:

> "We the people of the United States . . . do ordain and establish this Constitution. . . ."

In this abbreviated quotation from the preamble to our constitution, words are omitted in two places. Note the four dots at the second omission. Here the material left out would naturally complete the sentence, so the first dot is a period and the next three indicate omitted material.

THE EXCLAMATION POINT

Use the exclamation point (or mark) to emphasize an emotion or put starch into a command:

> I can't believe I ate the whole thing!

> "Drop the gat, Lefty, or I'll drill you!" shouted Scarlip O'Hara.

This mark is much beloved of high school sophomores. Experienced writers do not use it often because they consider it a substitute—and a poor one at that—for a well-chosen word. Never use two or more exclamation points together.

THE HYPHEN

Which statements are more likely to be true?

- **a**. Nice girls don't enter dirty movie theaters.
- **b**. Nice girls don't enter dirty-movie theaters.
- **c**. I saw a man eating lobster.
- **d**. I saw a man-eating lobster.

The answers are the second and third sentences; ah, the differences a little hyphen can make. Paradoxically, the two main purposes of this little mark are to join and to separate:

Use hyphens to join some compound words:

tongue-lashing   sit-in   has-been   user-friendly

The only way to be sure whether a compound should be written as one word *(bookcase)* or two words *(high school)* or hyphenated *(mother-in-law)* is to consult a current dictionary. Words that function as a compound adjective before a noun, however, are usually hyphenated. In such examples, the hyphens mirror the way one would speak the words, ensuring clarity and making reading easier:

one-night stand   state-of-the-art equipment
well-organized essay

We respectfully suggest that United Parcel Service and the U.S. Post Office would add zip to their "Next Day Air" and "Two Day Priority Mail" if they would switch to "Next-Day Air" and "Two-Day Priority Mail."

Use hyphens to join compound numbers less than one hundred and adjectival fractions:

> twenty-one   ninety-nine   one-eighth share

Use hyphens to separate prefixes from roots if two vowels of a small letter and a capital will otherwise run together:

> re-elect   anti-inflammatory   pre-eminent
>
> un-American   pre-Christmas   ex-President Carter

Use a hyphen to divide a word at the end of a line. Divide words by syllables; do not divide a one-syllable word, even if it ends in *-ed*.

PARENTHESES

Use parentheses to enclose an explanation or a statement that is not closely connected to the rest of the sentence. Parentheses offer a convenient way of inconspicuously adding a brief remark to help your readers understand your full meaning. Like dashes, parentheses normally imply a stronger interruption than commas used for the same purpose. Dashes tend to emphasize the interrupting element; parentheses tend to isolate it as an aside:

> Statesman and orator Daniel Webster (not to be confused with dictionary-maker Noah Webster) was the model of a story by Stephen Vincent Benét.

When the parenthetical element is part of a larger sentence, omit both the initial capital letter and the period within the parentheses. In such cases, marks of punctuation that belong to the sentence as a whole come outside the second curve. If the material within the parentheses is a separate sentence, start with an initial capital letter and supply final punctuation inside the second curve:

He was a gentleman (as his wife asserted), a scholar (if slightly pedantic), and an idealist (as he told me himself).

One reason linguists study Latin is that it is a "dead" language and therefore never changes. (Our English language, on the other hand, changes constantly.)

Use parentheses to enclose numbers or letters introducing parts of a series. Always use parentheses in pairs; a parenthesis looks lonely by itself:

The plaintiff has asked for (a) restitution for damages, (b) compensation for attorney's fees, and (c) written assurance that similar incidents will not occur again.

THE PERIOD

Other than to mark the end of a sentence, the only function of a period is to indicate abbreviation:

4:00 P.M.   Dr.   Ph.D.   Dec. 25

The period has been called the most underused punctuation mark, a reference to the fact that long, serpentine sentences are a common symptom of poor writing. Writing should not be all short, choppy sentences. Still, we recommend that, when you are in doubt, you should reach for a period instead of a semicolon or conjunction.

THE QUESTION MARK

Use a question mark after a direct question or to show that a statement of fact is open to question:

What is your reaction to the trade bill now being debated in Congress?

Geoffrey Chaucer (1340?–1400) was the first to write significant literature in English.

QUOTATION MARKS

Conversation adds life and interest to writing. Quotation marks help to make words talk. Their main purpose is to report what people say and write.

Use quotation marks to set off direct quotations:

In *Writing (Is an Unnatural Act)*, Professor James C. Raymond comments, "Punctuation . . . is one of those devices invented to translate words from a natural medium, the spoken language, to an artificial medium, writing."

Do not place quotation marks around indirect discourse or paraphrase:

She reported that the company was in good financial shape.

Confusion persists about the location of punctuation in relation to quotation marks. To banish such puzzlement, learn the following rules:

1. In American punctuation, periods and commas always—and we do mean always—go inside the quotation marks:

"The company is in good financial shape," she announced.

She announced, "The company is in good financial shape."

2. Semicolons always go outside quotation marks:

She announced, "The company is in good financial shape"; then she proceeded to cite figures that led to a different conclusion.

3. Question marks and exclamation marks go either inside or outside of the final quotation marks, depending on whether the question or exclamation is part of the quoted material:

She asked, "Is the company in good financial shape?"

Did you hear her announce, "The company is in good financial shape"?

Use single quotation marks to set off a quotation within a quotation:

"Perhaps the most quoted line in all of modern poetry," he said, "is T. S. Eliot's 'not with a bang but a whimper.'"

Use quotation marks to set off the titles of short works—poems, book chapters, magazine articles, short stories, and the like—that are usually included in longer works. Use italics (underlining on some keyboards) to indicate the titles of longer works—books, anthologies, magazines, motion pictures, operas, and the like:

In "The Art of Biography," published by the *Atlantic Monthly* for April 1939, Virginia Woolf argued that biography is a craft, not an art.

Use quotation marks (or italics) to distinguish words-as-words or to call attention to irony:

The word "indent" actually means "to take a bite out of."

The art and craft of writing is not simply something that an author can "give" and a reader "take." The reader must put the author's advice into practice.

But don't toss quotation marks around like rice at a wedding, or you may end up saying just the opposite of what you mean. "Fresh" fish is anything but fresh.

THE SEMICOLON

The semicolon has been described as a mark indicating a pause more strongly than would a comma and more weakly than would a period. Actually, most semicolons are closer to periods.

Use a semicolon to join closely related independent clauses:

> The would-be senator would tolerate no opposition; Wendy received notice of her dismissal the very next morning.

When the second clause is introduced by a conjunctive adverb, use a semicolon. Using a comma in such a situation results in a sentence error called a comma fault:

> The would-be senator asked for a free exchange of ideas; nevertheless, Wendy received notice of her dismissal the very next morning.

Not:

> The would-be senator asked for a free exchange of ideas, nevertheless, Wendy received notice of her dismissal the very next morning.

Use a semicolon as an extra-powerful comma before a coordinating conjunction joining clauses or between items of a series when the clauses or the items already contain commas.

This practice will help your readers to avoid confusion with other commas in the sentence.

When the second clause is introduced by a conjunction, you may use a comma, but sometimes the stronger break provided by the semicolon helps to clarify a sentence that contains several commas:

> The would-be senator emphasized team work, discussion, and a free exchange of ideas; yet Wendy received notice of her dismissal the very next morning.

> You learned in grammar school that a noun is a word that denotes a person, place, or thing; but you soon discovered that some nouns, such as *life, liberty,* and *happiness* transcend the three categories you were taught.

Test Yourself

To take an inventory of your control of the marks from commas to semicolons, from quotation marks to parentheses, correct the sentences below. Some of them contain unnecessary or incorrect punctuation; others omit punctuation that should be used:

1. Margaret Mitchell, author of "Gone with the Wind," was a native of Georgia, however, she became known throughout the world.

2. The company has offices in Atlanta, Georgia, Tacoma, Washington, Birmingham, Alabama, and San Juan, Puerto Rico.

3. Sally is ten years old, her brother is only three.

4. Before he came to the company he founded another company that manufactured the same products.

5. Let's eat Herman; I'm starved said Carlito.

6. December 7, 1941 is known as "Pearl Harbor Day". President Franklin Roosevelt who called it a day that will live in infamy died before the end of the war.

7. I have nothing to offer but blood, toil, tears and sweat, said Winston Churchill the great "World War II" leader.

8. The student asked, "Who was it who wrote, all the world's a stage and all the men and women merely players"?

9. In army slang, a shavetail is a second lieutenant. The company commander is often referred to as the old man. I was a 22 year old shavetail, and was briefly company commander. I often wondered whether the men in my company most of whom were older than I called me the old man.

10. That that is is that that is not is not.

─────── ANSWERS ───────

1. Margaret Mitchell, author of *Gone with the Wind*, was a native of Georgia; however, she became known throughout the world.

2. The company has offices in Atlanta, Georgia; Tacoma, Washington; Birmingham, Alabama; and San Juan, Puerto Rico.

3. Sally is ten years old; her brother is only three.

4. Before he came to the company, he founded another company that manufactured the same products.

5. "Let's eat, Herman; I'm starved," said Carlito.

6. December 7, 1941, is known as Pearl Harbor Day. President Franklin Roosevelt, who called it "a day that will live in infamy," died before the end of the war.

7. "I have nothing to offer but blood, toil, tears, and sweat," said Winston Churchill, the great World War II leader.

8. The student asked, "Who was it who wrote, 'All the world's a stage, and all the men and women merely players'?"

9. In army slang, a "shavetail" is a second lieutenant. The company commander is often referred to as "the old man." I was a 22-year-old shavetail and was briefly a company commander. I often wondered whether the men in my company—most of whom were older than I—called me the old man.

10. That that is, is; that that is not, is not.

TEST YOURSELF (ONE LAST TIME)

Now we provide no punctuation and ask you to provide all necessary marks. Keep each statement as a single sentence:

1. The Bible which is the central book in religious thought speaks of three virtues faith hope and charity and says the greatest of these is charity

2. Did James travel all the way to Concord New Hampshire to look for the Joneses first edition copy of the story The Tell-Tale Heart he asked

3. Did Julie really declare I refuse to make my bed and I shall never again wash dishes vacuum rugs or water plants asked Jenny

4. Although the school is again warning Mary its warned her many times before the brave wonderfully coordinated young woman wants to try out for the boys football team.

5. Roosevelt brilliantly exploited the political situation by bringing together five have not entities the South which had lived for years in a state of chronic depression Roosevelt was to characterize it as the countrys number one economic problem the Roman Catholics who still formed a minority group in many parts of the country the blacks particularly those settled in the urban communities the Jews and the labor unions (from Brooks Lewis and Warren American Literature The Makers and the Making)

ANSWERS

1. The Bible, which is the central book in religious thought, speaks of three virtues—faith, hope, and charity—and says that the greatest of these is charity.

(Commas to separate the nonrestrictive adjective clause; double dashes to set off compound appositive that contains commas for noun series.)

2. "Did James travel all the way to Concord, New Hampshire, to look for the Joneses' first-edition copy of the story 'The Tell-Tale Heart'?" he asked.

(Quotation marks for quotation; comma after *New Hampshire*, as well as before; apostrophe after *Joneses*; hyphen for *first-edition* as a compound adjective; single quotation marks for the short-story title set within double quotation marks; question mark outside the single quotation marks; period, not question mark, at end of sentence.)

3. "Did Julie really declare, 'I refuse to make my bed; and I shall never again wash dishes, vacuum rugs, or water plants!'?" asked Jenny.

(Quotation marks for quotation; single quotation marks within double quotation marks; semicolon before *and* to separate two independent clauses one of which contains commas for the verb series; exclamation mark before single quotation mark ending quotation, and question mark before the double quotation mark; period, not question mark, at end of sentence.)

4. Although the school is again warning Mary (it's warned her many times before), the brave, wonderfully coordinated girl wants to try out for the boys' [or *boys*] football team.

(Parentheses for parenthetical sentence in the middle of a larger sentence; *it's* as a contraction; comma after second parenthesis to set off introductory adverb clause; comma for adjective series.)

5. Roosevelt brilliantly exploited the political situation by bringing together five have-not entities—the South, which had lived for years in a state of chronic depression (Roosevelt was to characterize it as the country's number one economic problem); the Roman Catholics, who still formed a minority group in many parts of the country; the blacks, particularly those settled in urban communities; the Jews; and the labor unions. (from Brooks, Lewis, and Warren, *American Literature: The Makers and the Making)*

(Hyphen for compound modifier; dash to set off compound appositive; commas to set off nonrestrictive adjective clauses; parentheses to set off parenthetical statement within the larger sentence; semicolons to set off series in which one or more noun phrase contains commas; commas for series of authors; book title italicized or underlined.)

A Glossary of Terms

"Every self-respecting mechanic," wrote John Dewey, "will call the parts of an automobile by their right names because that is the way to distinguish them." Similarly, the ability to name the moving and movable parts of a statement helps the writer to perceive the almost infinite variety of the English sentence. Here, then, is a naming of the parts:

Active voice   The verb form in which the doer is the subject of the action. Opposed to **passive voice**, the verb form in which the subject receives the action.

Adjective   A word that describes or limits a noun or pronoun. An adjective tells which one, what kind of, or how many.

Adverb   A word that modifies a verb, adjective, another adverb, or the whole clause of a sentence. An adverb tells how, when, or where. English adverbs frequently, but not always, end in -*ly*.

Agreement   Two words or more agree when they are cast in the same person, number, case, or gender.

Antecedent   The word, phrase, or clause to which a pronoun refers.

Appositive   A noun or noun cluster that is set alongside a first noun or pronoun to explain it more fully.

Article   *A, an* **(indefinite articles)**, and *the* **(definite article)** point out any one of a group of nouns.

Case   The form of a pronoun that indicates its function. English has three cases: **nominative case** (sometimes called **subjective**), **objective case** (sometimes called **accusative**), and **possessive** (sometimes called **genitive**).

Clause   A group of words that contains a subject and a verb. A clause may be **independent** (able to stand alone; sometimes called **main**) or **dependent** (also called **subordinate**). In terms of function, clauses may act as **adjective clauses**, **adverb clauses**, or **noun clauses**.

Collective noun   A noun that is singular in form names a group of people or things.

Compound elements   A **compound sentence** contains two or more independent clauses linked by a conjunction or a semicolon. A **compound subject** consists of two or more nouns or pronouns linked by a coordinating conjunction to form the subject of one verb. A **compound verb** consists of two or more verbs that share the same subject.

Conjunction   A word or words that join words, phrases, or clauses. Conjunctions may be **coordinating**, **subordinating**, or **correlative**.

Connotation   The shade of meaning of a word beyond its **denotation**, dictionary definition.

Gender   The masculine, feminine, or neuter characteristics of words.

Gerund   A verb form ending in *-ing* and used as a noun.

Idiom   A combination of words that native speakers of a language accept as natural and correct even though it does not follow usual patterns of construction or usage.

Infinitive   The basic form of a verb, usually preceded by *to*.

Mood   The attitude toward a statement or question. The verb forms used in sentences about actual things and events are cast in the **indicative mood**. Those used in sentences containing conditions contrary to fact or highly doubtful, wishes, and various idioms are cast in the **subjunctive mood**.

Modifiers   Words or groups of words that describe or restrict other words. **Misplaced** or **dangling modifiers** wreck the scaffolding of a sentence.

Noun   The name of a person, place, thing, or idea.

Object   The term applied to a noun or pronoun that receives the action of a verb—and is thus a **direct object** or **indirect object**—or comes at the end of a prepositional phrase—and is thus an **object of a preposition**.

Parallelism   The stylistic device of expressing equally important thoughts in parallel grammatical forms.

Participle   A verb form ending in *-ing*, *-ed*, *-en*, or *-t* used as an adjective.

Phrase   A group of words without a subject and predicate that functions as a single part of speech in a sentence.

Predicate   The main verb in a clause or sentence and all its modifiers and objects. Together, these tell what the subject is doing or how it is existing.

Preposition   A word indicating movement, direction, location, or relationship that links a noun or pronoun to the rest of the sentence. Every preposition takes an object.

Pronoun   A word that takes the place of a noun. Pronouns are classified as **personal**, **indefinite**, **demonstrative**, and **interrogative**. A pronoun must agree with its antecedent and clearly refer to that antecedent. Otherwise, **ambiguous** or **vague reference** results.

Proper noun   In contrast to a **common noun**, the capitalized name of a particular person, place, thing, or idea.

Redundancy   An unnecessary repetition of meaning. Also known as **pleonasm**.

Restrictive element   An appositive, phrase, or clause that, unlike a **nonrestrictive element**, identifies that which it modifies by telling which particular person or thing is meant.

Sentence   A unit of words containing a subject and predicate that in writing begins with a capital letter and ends with appropriate punctuation. Classified by purpose, sentences may be **declarative**, **imperative**, **interrogative**, or **exclamatory**.

Sentence errors   When writers connect two sentences by a comma, they create a **comma splice**. When writers join two sentences with no punctuation at all, they create a **run-on sentence**. A part of a sentence detached from the whole and punctuated as a separate sentence is a **sentence fragment**.

Singular   The quality of a noun, pronoun, or verb that refers to one element, as opposed to **plural**, the quality of a noun, pronoun, or verb that refers to more than one.

Syntax   The arrangement of grammatical elements in a sentence to create meaning.

Subject   The noun or pronoun that a clause or sentence is about. The "who or what" of a verb.

Tense   The form of a verb that shows the time of its action. The six tenses in English are **present, past, future, present perfect, past perfect**, and **future perfect**.

Verb   Every sentence must contain, expressed or implied, a verb—a word that expresses action or being. Categories include **transitive verbs**, which take objects to complete their meaning; **intransitive verbs**, which do not take objects; and **linking verbs** (usually forms of *to be*), which link a subject with a **predicate noun** or **predicate adjective**.

Recommended Reading

Any good worker needs good tools and the knowledge of how to use them. Carpenters rely on hammer and nails, saw and wood, and plumb bob and square; dancers on pointe shoes and rosin, leotard and tutu, and barre and mirrors.

Centuries ago, poet Alexander Pope reminded us that, like dancers, writers can master their art and craft through practice:

> *True ease in writing comes from art, not chance,*
> *As those move easiest who have learned to dance.*

To help you "move easiest" through your life as a worker with words, we offer a short, highly selective reading list. We believe that these books can help you to set pen to paper and fingers to keyboard with greater confidence and authority.

Bernstein, Theodore M. *The Careful Writer.* New York: Atheneum, 1980. The best and most comprehensive of Bernstein's usage books, this volume contains careful explanations, sound reasoning, and delightful humor.

Chicago Editorial Staff. *The Chicago Manual of Style,* 14th ed. Chicago: University of Chicago Press, 1993. One of a number of comprehensive style manuals, this is the most universally used of style elbow books.

Follett, Wilson. *Modern American Usage*. New York: Hill & Wang, 1966.

Fowler, H. W. *A Dictionary of Modern English Usage*, 2nd ed., revised. London: Oxford University Press, 1987. Follett's and Fowler's idiosyncratic and comprehensive elbow books are two classics in the field of usage.

Johnson, Edward D. *The Handbook of Good English*. New York: Washington Square Press, 1991. This is a marvelously thorough handbook that provides authoritative answers to questions about grammar, usage, and punctuation.

Kilpatrick, James J. *The Writer's Art*. Kansas City: Andrews and McMeel, 1985. The widely syndicated columnist on the art of writing has outdone himself in writing this one. Kilpo's love of language constantly illuminates his sage words about the art of writing.

Merriam-Webster's Dictionary of English Usage. Springfield, Mass.: Merriam-Webster, Inc., 1993, revised ed. Clearly and readably, the articles in this nearly one-thousand-page guide examine all the main issues of American usage. Exhaustive, but not at all exhausting.

Morris, William, and Mary Morris. *Harper Dictionary of Contemporary Usage*, 2nd ed. New York: Harper & Row, 1992. An especially valuable usage manual because it includes comments by the Harper usage panel of experts.

Strunk, William, Jr., and E. B. White, *The Elements of Style*, 3rd ed. New York: Macmillan, 1979. This classic book on writing, style, and usage proves the adage that great things come in small packages.

Tarshis, Barry. *Grammar for Smart People*. New York: Pocket Books, 1993. Snappy and accurate answers to your questions about usage, punctuation, and spelling, especially for businesspeople.

Zinsser, William. *On Writing Well*, 4th ed. New York: Harper & Row, 1993. The former newspaperman writes wondrously well when he writes on writing well.

About SPELL

SPELL, the Society for the Preservation of English Language and Literature, is a nonprofit organization that promotes high standards of English. Founded in 1984 by a retired advertising executive, SPELL now has members throughout the United States and Canada. They include writers, editors, teachers, students, attorneys, physicians, engineers, executives, secretaries, homemakers, and retired persons—a diverse group of people bound together by their love of English and their determination to resist its abuse and misuse by inept writers and speakers in the news media and elsewhere. Members use SPELL's increasingly familiar and respected Goof Cards to cite such errors and offer constructive criticism. The organization also sponsors an annual scholarship-essay contest for high school students.

SPELL's entertaining and informative newsletter, *SPELL/Binder*, carries articles on writing, usage, grammar, and other language-related subjects. Contributors include the authors of this book and other nationally known writers.

Financial support for SPELL comes from donations, bequests, and membership fees. Membership is open to anyone who supports SPELL's main objective. The cost is $20 for the first year and $15 annually thereafter. Please write to:

SPELL
P.O. Box 118
Waleska, GA 30183